THE BUMBLE BEE IN ME
Living the Ironman Dream
YEE SZE MUN

"It is not what you are born with. It is how you deal with your life. Think like a Bumble Bee. Follow your dream."

© Yee Sze Mun 2016

Published by
Yee Sze Mun
36, Jalan TR 8/2
Mukim Damansara
Petaling Jaya
47410 Selangor
Malaysia

ISBN: 978-967-14435-0-7

All rights reserved. No part of this publication may be reproduced or transmitted in any form or by any means, electronic or mechanical, including photocopy, recording or any information storage and retrieval system, without permission in writing from the copyright owners.

Images on the cover page, title page, pages 149, 150 and inside back cover used with permission from Ironman Malaysia.

Book art direction and design by Joyce Yee.
Printed by CreateSpace.

CONTENTS

Acknowledgements   vii
Foreword   ix

Chapter 1: This 'addiction' beats me up, yet I keep coming back for more...
My longest day   2

Chapter 2: From where I came...
Queen of Hearts, a tribute to 'Po Kee' Ah Ma   21
Family history from Malaysia to China   24
Shantou detour – An emotional wound   27

Chapter 3: The price of climbing the corporate ladder
Playing catch-up – the fast track education lane   33
Joining the workforce – learning all the way   36
A life changing transition – the wake up call   38

Chapter 4: Life changes at 50
A humbling experience – Three little girls and a foolish me   43
Accidental initiation – Back on the saddle with the tricky pedals   48
Swim, Bike, Run – My first Triathlon   52
Unpredictable tides – Kapas to Marang Swimathon   56

Chapter 5: You are never too old to take on new challenges
Improving with age   61
Taking on Marathon des Sables   66
The M Dot – my priceless beauty   80
2001 National Geographic Action Asia Challenge   87
2002 National Geographic Action Asia Challenge (Take 2 – The Three Stooges)   90
The 8th Asian Triathlon Championship, July 11th, 1999 – Korea   103

Chapter 6: Lessons in life, training and the power of friendly competition

Tomo and me	107
To beat Old Man Yee	118
My golden years	123
The long journey	127
Lessons in humanity	136
Father time	140
Wake-up! Doubting Thomases – Anything is possible	142

Epilogue   146

Acknowledgements

My heart is racing, breathing is fast and shallow and the damn leg muscles are burning as I grind up the steepest climb at the start of the bike leg in my second attempt of the Ironman World Championships in Kona, Hawaii, 1996. When I finally make it to the top of Palani Road I am light headed and my vision a little blurred. I have difficulty balancing on my bike and am forced to dismount just in time to throw up my breakfast. Giving up would be the easy option but being the stubborn Ox I am, quitting is not an option. The same fainting spell hits me twice more during the bike leg and I end up missing the cut off by just 7 minutes or 420 seconds. Whichever way you look at it, it doesn't soften the disappointment about receiving a DNF (Did Not Finish). It was and still is to date my only DNF in six attempts of the Ironman World Championships.

My gym mates all think I should write a book on my exploits, achievements, highs and lows. They wonder how I can be so positive all of the time. How am I able to joke and laugh at my misadventures and miseries?

My family members, though proud of my achievements have no idea of my long journey to the start of each race. The ordeal I go through getting to each and every finish line and my feelings once I get there, and the ultimate question – why am I still chasing the same dream at the ripe old age of 79?

Putting my experiences onto paper may serve as a life lesson to their children and their children's children. It will (I hope) teach that in life, 'Anything is Possible' as proven by their grand and great grand pa.

This book would not be complete without acknowledgements and thanks to those who have had a hand in making me what I am today. My love to my mum, Chew Po Kee, a great mother, a tough and resilient woman, I am pleased to say I have been blessed with some of her good genes.

My first boss, Tony Godwin (now deceased) showed me what makes a good leader. Lead and advise from the front, do not shout orders from the back and never tolerate the same mistake twice.

K.W. Yeow, my ex-colleague who drummed into me 'work will not kill a person but worries do'.

Mark Snyders who picked and gave me my first jump in my career by just observing the ways I conducted myself in performing my duties.

C.J. Boyles (now deceased) my MD who despite his doubts about "a China Man who can hardly speak English," gave me an opportunity in life.

Ling Lar Tine, my ex-secretary for her patience in tirelessly typing and retyping my scripts over and over again.

Miss Emma Bishop for helping out with the initial edit and arrangement.

Bob Holmes for helping out with the final edit of the book.

Geoff Meyer for writing a foreword capturing the spirit of IRONMAN.

Jonathan Tan and Bob Holmes for writing encouraging endorsements of the book.

Encik Mohd. Tazidi bin Yusof for the illustrations that brought my stories to life.

My daughter, Joyce who helped with the design, layout and art direction of the book.

And finally, thanks to US Navy commander John Collins, as the creator of the Ironman. Big John, like for so many others, started my dream. He gave me hope. Without the Ironman, I might not be what I am today and these words may never have been written.

It is my hope that you will enjoy these stories, be inspired and truly believe anything is possible.

Yee Sze Mun
16 times Ironman finisher

Foreword

When I was asked to write a foreword to Mr Yee's book "The Bumble Bee in Me", I was very much honoured to do so. I thought though what do I say, Mr Yee has achieved so much and still is, 16 IRONMAN finishers, five of which were the IRONMAN World Championships Kailua Kona Hawaii, over 35 IRONMAN 70.3's and all at an extraordinary age. We at IRONMAN owe Mr Yee so much, he has done a lot to put IRONMAN not only on the Malaysian but global map, with his large following worldwide, a true IRONMAN ambassador and icon of our sport. Mr Yee epitomises the IRONMAN spirit, strength, endurance, a never give up attitude and yes he is the definition of "anything is possible"

This is only part of what makes up Mr Yee, yes a formidable athlete in his own right but to me it's the energy Mr Yee exudes! It's a positive, friendly, warm, welcoming, very young at heart passion that is second to none. That is Mr Yee! I travel to many, many IRONMAN events around the globe and I always know when Mr Yee is there because the energy that he radiates is there well before him. We by nature are a fairly uptight athletic community worrying about everything, have I done enough training, have I done too much, is my nutrition right? Mr Yee walks in and there is a calm that comes across the transition and everyone smiles and remembers why they are there, what brought them, yes the challenge but to enjoy, to have fun, to feed off that positive energy and enjoy that journey to the finish line with like-minded people. Whether Mr Yee has a good or bad day that positive energy is still there for everyone to share, even better if its with two of his favourites, a beer, good seafood and maybe another beer.

Mr Yee our first inductee into the Malaysian Hall of Fame is truly a gentleman, a family man that has my full respect, I know you will enjoy his tales and I very much look forward to many more to come.

Geoff Meyer
Managing Director, IRONMAN® Asia

CHAPTER 1

This 'addiction' beats me up, yet I keep coming back for more...

My longest day

Swim start of my first Hawaii Ironman, 1995.

My watch says 6:45am and I am standing on the pier in Kailua Kona, a little seaside town in the Big Island of Hawaii. It is October 7, 1995 and the sun has just broken through on distant horizon over the vast Pacific Ocean. Giant floodlights illuminate the pier and surrounding area that is abuzz with thousands of people. Among the volunteers, staff and spectators are over 1500 of the world's fittest athletes waiting to face their longest day. I stand among them, not feeling quite like I completely belong. The atmosphere is electric; my heart is in my throat. I just want to get my day started.

Booming over the loudspeaker the emcee, the Voice of Ironman announces the countdown is on, "We are 15 minutes from the start of the race of your life."

There are a handful of steps leading down 'Dig Me' beach that can hold no more than 100 people. Athletes are queued all the way back down along the pier waiting their turn to enter. It is high tide and those daring spectators that have taken up prime spot on the sea wall are subjected to a soaking every time a large wave crashes into the wall.

Athletes slowly push forwards. Less then 20 metres of hard packed sand offers a final taste of terraferma before we are herded forwards into the beckoning waves of the Pacific.

It is finally my turn to enter the beach. Balancing on submerged rocks in front of the sea wall is myself, a nervous little rookie waiting for the starting cannon to boom. Butterflies swarm in my stomach. "This is so scary!" How do I cope with a stampede of 3000 pairs of thrashing limbs?

Despite having some experience with open water swimming, this is my first encounter swimming with so many people, so many fast people. Suddenly I doubt myself, I feel my resolve weakening before I even begin. Adding a further blow to my growing concerns, fellow Malaysian, Mohammed Sofian, finds me and delivers a lasting blow.

"*Mr Yee! Are you sure you can do it?*"

Sofian is in the prime of his life and has completed the race before. His question was the last thing I was expecting. Some words of wisdom, encouragement perhaps, but not a deafening punch of "Are you sure you can do this?"

Suddenly an eerie silence falls on proceedings as 100 metres out in the ocean professional athletes are lined up, treading water awaiting the starting cannon with the United States national anthem. The cannon sounds and the day starts. I must forget my doubts, rid the words of Sofian from my mind and start my longest day.

In 1995 the Ironman brand was still in its infancy. The World Championships had yet to take hold of the hearts and minds of athletes around the world. It was because of this fact that I was able to enter simply by writing a letter and requesting an entry. I was not here because of my athletic ability. I was one of three Malaysians who gained entry by application. I had the desire and I had the balls to ask! With that in mind I was 58 years old and had absolutely zero background in any of the swim, bike and run disciplines.

As the cannon sounds my mind is jolted awake to a whirl of self-doubt, anticipation, fear and excitement. I have just stepped down onto the beach and am moving forward when a wave smashes me back against the sea wall. I come to; goggles askew, shaken and disorientated but thankfully not hurt. By the time I recover from the shock and begin swimming I notice I am the last one to leave the shore. My fellow athletes are now some meters ahead, caught in the biggest white water fury of kicking legs and propeller of arms I have ever encountered.

I take my time to ease into rhythm and recall a mantra from the third member of our Malaysian team, Chan Chee Seng. "You are not here to compete with the others. Take it easy. Take one leg at a time." With Chee Seng's more helpful words of advice echoing in my mind, that is precisely what I do.

The Hawaii Ironman swim start is known as the world's largest washing machine. Immediately following the boom of the starting cannon, more than 3000 pairs of limbs begin moving at once in tandem, fighting for a space, that is not there. Only the strongest swimmers get

This 'addiction' beats me up, yet I keep coming back for more…

to take the straightest line. If you get caught in the midst of this human washing machine, for a newbie such as myself it is a living hell. Through my own 'luck' of getting struck by a wave I may be last to start but at least I am clear of the tundra of flailing limbs.

I constantly remind myself that I am competing against only myself. Once I get into my swim rhythm, my heart rate steadies and I allow myself to enjoy the remaining 3.8km.

The water surrounding the Big Island is crystal blue. The seabed is formed by lava and colonized by a variety of colourful corals; clearly visible are schools of tropical fish. Beneath the kicking feet atop the water, TV crews in vivid wetsuits lay on the seabed to capture the fury above.

I fall into a steady pace following bobbing orange markers. Every now and then I catch up with a fellow athlete and overtake them. I even try my skill at drafting the tail of small groups of swimmers I come upon. It helps to conserve some energy, energy that I know I will need to draw on on later in the day.

Two tour boats are anchored at the swim turnaround. On board are race officials, photographers and some spectators. It is here where the water becomes a little rougher as athletes try to round the boats as tightly as possible and save distance. Once I have made it safely round the packs began to stretch out again. I am on my way home; Dig Me Beach a far speck on the horizon is my goal. Relaxed and calm I enjoy the return to the pier much more than the swim out and reach 'home' in 1 hour and 33 minutes. 7 minutes faster than my anticipated time. "Who said this Ironman thing is a survival test?" I feel great!

The 180km bike leg begins from a car park on the pier. I get changed and head out of transition to begin what I know will be a long day in the saddle. Immediately 200 meters out from the pier I am faced with a steep slow climb up Palani Drive, also known as the 'Pay N Save hill'. The hill stretches out ahead of me for 1km and in no time at all I am tested. My cycling legs are still a work in progress and with my heart rate shooting through the roof I try to turn wobbly swim legs into bike legs pedalling in a ski slope fashion up the hill. I so badly want to get down and push my bike up the damn hill but ego is a wonderful thing and does not allow me to. With thousands of spectators cheering athletes on, how can I walk?

Starting my bike leg of the race. Little did I realise what was in store for me.

The shouts work their magic and I am able to get out of my saddle and force a slow grind to the top. Two hours ago the professionals no doubt had made light work of ascending Palani, my respect for their seemingly superhuman abilities is amplified as I reach the top and realize I still have 179km to go.

In ten long minutes my ego and cockiness over my sense of good feeling after the swim is laid to rest. My heart is now once again in my throat and so are those doubting Thomases. I had an uneasy feeling I would be fighting with Thomas for the rest of the day.

Hawaii is a tropical island paradise. While on a trip to the US mainland during the early 80's, I stopped over in Honolulu for a couple of days and really enjoyed the beauty of the island and was keen to make a return trip at some point later in life. It took almost a quarter of century to realize that dream. This time my destination was the Big Island of Kona where I would be racing my first Ironman.

As the plane was approaching Kona airport I looked out of the window expecting to see beautiful palm tree lined beaches, blue lagoons a la Honolulu. I could not believe my eyes when all I saw was a landscape that had more in common with the craters of the moon than the idyllic postcard scenes I had stored in my mind for 25 years. The land was completely barren, uninhabitable charcoal black lava rock. What on earth were organizers thinking of to arrange a race on such a desolate godforsaken place!

At the top of Palani I make a left turn towards the Queen Kaahumanu Highway aka Queen K. From there I have 13km of rolling hills towards the Keahole airport. There is an ocean breeze blowing on my left across the Queen K at a gentle 16-20kph. Progressing with an average speed of 27kph, a little faster than my normal speed, I start thinking that I can complete the bike leg in about seven hours and change leaving me plenty of time to run the marathon. Despite it being so early in the day I was once again getting carried away with my thoughts rather than focusing on the job in hand. I had no idea how fast things can change out in the lava fields. I also had no idea how my inexperienced green credentials would be put to the test.

Naïve to the journey ahead, believing I had this in the bag I carry on buoyed with this new knowledge and renewed confidence that I would get a decent bike split. My newfound confidence is short lived and I am reminded of why this is a world championship soon after passing the airport. 'Mumuku' the legendary wind of Hawaii, raises her head.

"Welcome to the twilight zone my friend your nightmare has begun."

The Queen K is about 128km long and two lanes wide. Carved from lava fields it is jet black, sizzling hot and home to shifting winds and long rolling hills. It runs through some of the most hostile landscape on earth. Nothing grows on this arid landscape except for a few scattered brave bougainvillea that add a dash of contrasting colour to the road shoulder. It is a desert with no sand; lava rock is the choice element. The Queen K is the main battlefield of Ironman Hawaii, the anvil against which Ironman World Championship hopefuls are shaped into their dreams or beaten into submission. Athletes must bike the entire length of the highway twice and then to rub a little more salt into the wounds, 25km of the marathon will take athletes back out on to the highway. Those who survive are the ones who can better deal with the elements thrown at them during the bike course. To many, the Queen K is where Ironman dreams are made and lost.

The winds on October 7, 1995 were some of the worst to date. Mumuku was merciless that day. She constantly hammered athletes on the bike with 50kph plus headwinds and unpredictable gusts of crosswinds over 90kph.

I am making slow progress on the flat stretches of the highway. The rolling hills offer no respite and the whole process very quickly turns from 'I can do this' to a huge ordeal; a laborious chore that I am not enjoying. When I reach the tops of the rolling hills there is no relief, the wind is blowing head on and if I don't keep pedalling to maintain a pathetic speed of 12-13kph I will go nowhere. It is completely demoralizing and if that wasn't enough I have to utilize even more of my precious energy to control my bike against the crosswinds and stay upright. For the very first time in my life, I am fearful of riding my bike. I can only compare it to that of riding a bull at a rodeo.

I am so scared that I dare not lift my hand off the bars to shift gears. When I do need to change gear I stop the bike, get down and do it manually then climb back on and off I go again. The ego that kept me from getting off the bike and walking up Palani a couple of hours ago is long gone. I am in survival mode, but also there is no one here in this barren land to make me think otherwise and suck it up and just change the damn gear like normal. I soon realize this tactic is not helping my diminishing confidence, so I leave the bike in the lightest gear and pedal albeit, slowly along.

It is important to eat while on the bike, to keep energy levels up. Eating on the move is not always a smooth process. I took advice to cut my energy bars into strips and adhere them to the top tube of my bike. Not knowing any difference, the green athlete in me listened to this 'advice'. By the time I am ready to take my first 'fuel' strip the sun, beating down, had beaten me to it. The bar, or the remains of the bar were nothing but a sticky gooey mess. As panic starts to rise in my throat I quickly counter that my only option is to stop and refuel at all the aid stations.

Hawi marks the bike course turnaround. Before reaching this point there is a gradual hill, 16km long. The strong headwind is pushing me backwards as I try my hardest to make progress forwards. It is the longest and most painful 16km I have ever endured, and I take over an hour to reach the top.

There is little relief waiting for me when I reach the turnaround. For once again there is 16km of descending laid out in front of me. I watch in awe as other more competent riders fly past at breakneck speeds making the most of this 'free speed'. There is no free speed and no rest for myself; the crosswinds are still howling trying to make me a casualty. My 16km decent turns into a white-knuckle ride with my hands constantly on the brakes, trying to stay upright.

I reach the bottom unscathed and breathe a sigh of relief. It is short-lived and my nightmare takes on a new character in the form of a furnace. Since there is no more wind to disguise the searing heat I am now riding under the relentless sun with no shade and no wind to cool me down. My race number is minute-by-minute burning deeper into my skin by the sun's rays and my backside is on fire from saddle sores from sweat that is draining through my padded swim trunks onto raw skin (this was back in the day before tri-suits became available). If one believes in hell then I am definitely in the right place. I have no idea how long the stretch of highway out in front of me is, all I know is it is never ending. I grit my teeth and carry on wishing for some wind to come and rescue me from this discomfort.

No sooner have these thoughts passed through my mind I find myself lying on the hot black asphalt. A sudden gust of wind has swept my bike and me up and thrown us across the road, past the hard shoulder where we have settled in a heap at the guardrail. Lying there in a daze I hear the ensuing conversation between the Hawaii's two mythical Goddesses.

Mdm. Pele: "This chap slipped through my net, fix him."

Mdm. Mumuku: "No worries. Leave him with me."

Mumuku turns to me, "Welcome to my wind tunnel! You want to be an Ironman? Then show me what you are made of!"

I may be down but I am by no means out. No one will stop me. If I have to push my bike all the way to the finish line, I will. With the exception of some minor cuts and bruises I am not hurt. I pick myself up, get back on my bike and continue on into the nightmare of the Queen K.

In the morning, trade winds blow from the Pacific towards the mountains. It changes direction in the afternoon and blows back from the mountains to the Pacific. This means that many age group athletes, myself included have to battle headwinds in both directions. This is a cruel penalty for being a slower athlete.

Now the fun does not stop there for us mere mortals. Throw in unpredictable crosswinds, turn up the heat and add in the hills - then the Queen K becomes the perfect battleground to eke out the weak from the strong. The heat at noon is fierce and the return leg is strewn with battered bodies and souls fighting to survive. Choosing to drop out of the race is no longer a choice for many and one by one I see the Queen K take her share of victims who no longer have the will nor the strength to continue.

Just when I thought my day could not get any worse Mumuku sweeps me off my bike for a second time. And once again it is the guardrail that saves me from being swallowed up by a rocky ravine. I rally again and get back on my bike with the sounds of sirens ringing in my ears from emergency response units collecting less fortunate casualties. Despite my pain and agony I am not giving up. Quitting is not in my vocabulary. I struggle on, hoping and praying the worst of the winds have finally passed.

I have just passed the airport, heading back towards town and notice I am no longer alone. The Queen K is suddenly alive with runners on both sides of the highway. Some athletes are making the turnaround at the Energy Lab and are just about to enter the lonely stretch of sizzling lava beds. Others are heading home towards the finish line. I notice some running, some walking and there are also quite a few just sitting or lying down at the side of the highway. Their bodies fatigued, their day has come to a premature end with dreams in tatters for another year.

The sight of those broken spirits and bodies turns my relief at nearing Palani and the end of my treacherous bike ride into serious worry. Irrespective of their physical condition these athletes in front of me can take comfort that they are on the last leg of their longest day. I still have 25km on this damn bike before I can even contemplate joining them on the run course. A little voice within reminds me to push harder if I am to realize the hope of joining them. I push as hard as I physically can for the remaining stretch to transition, at the end of Alii Drive, 16km north of Kona. I look at my watch at realize with horror and growing panic that I only have 45 minutes to spare before bike cut-off at 5:30pm.

I am finally just 2km away and desperately want to take it easy and spin my legs; save something for the marathon but what lies ahead is the steepest hill. It is the last hurdle of this sadistic bike course that nearly breaks me.

Half way up the hill my legs finally give up and my wheels stop rolling. I get off and push my bike the rest of the way to the top of the hill. The ego that kept me on my bike earlier that morning is long gone. At the top of the hill I get back on and am finally able to coast down Palani all the way to transition. I cross the timing point in a time of 8 hours 59 minutes and 26 seconds. I make the cut-off by a whisker but there is no relief to be had. The bike has sucked every last ounce of energy from my battered body and I still have a marathon to complete.

I enter transition and go into the change tent to get ready for the marathon. My body is tired but my mind is fully alert. I have survived the toughest leg of this race; I now have six and a half hours to complete the marathon. I can do that. I CAN do that, this is the mantra I carry with me as I set out once again onto Alii Drive and the final leg of my longest day.

Once again I have underestimated this day. Thinking that the worst is behind me and I 'just' have to do a marathon is a very naïve move. Out there in the lava fields there is a large slice of humble pie waiting for me.

In an Ironman the swim is a warm up. The bike (for me) is tiring. The marathon is where it counts. The marathon is where your race is won or lost. As I head out from T2 in the car park of the Kona Surf Hotel and Resort at the bottom of Alii Drive I manage to shuffle my body up the hill despite a pair of legs that are refusing to cooperate. I am moving as though stuck in concrete. I carry on, hoping that my bike legs will turn into the running legs I so desperately now need. I reach the top of the road and then follow the course into an area known as 'the pit'. I reach the bottom, my legs shaky from the steep descent and then drag myself all the way up the next hill. I am now walking. It is my only option, there is no shame in it and I see many others doing the same.

The hills give way to flat roads and my body finally starts to feel like a runner and I find myself running along a residential road with the ocean on my left as I enter into Kailua-Kona. The sun is setting and the temperature has lowered enough to provide a light early evening breeze to soothe both mind and body. Whereas the bike was a lonely affair and a true battle of my mental strength the run course along the coastline is deep with spectators. For a while my spirits are lifted with the help of residents and hotel guests who stand by the roadside cheering their support. Some even set up tables and chairs, enjoying snacks and drinks as they watch the drama unfold. A few even bring out garden hoses to spray water over the athletes. The terrain during this 16km stretch is mostly flat, my pain has subsided and I find I am able to manage a jog between aid stations. As I return into Kona, it is already dark but I know I have made good progress. Before I head back out a volunteer pins a glow stick to the front and back of my vest. I am about to head out onto the darkest and loneliest stage of the marathon.

As I approach the 'Pay and Save' hill at Palani, the same damn hill I battled up on the bike hours earlier I see my wife. Despite her shouts of encouragement I can only walk up that hill. I know that ahead of me, the Queen K is waiting. 11km along on the Queen K, I am directed down towards the Energy Lab, a lonely dark out and back. Temperatures in the daytime sizzle. I can thank my lucky stars the heat has subsided, but as I shuffle along down the dark lonely road into a black hole of darkness I have a new concern, time.

It is 9:15pm and I have made it to the Energy Lab junction. I have so far covered 29km of the marathon. Having survived the high winds and heat of the elements all day long, my body has little left to give this day. If you are able to defeat the winds of the Queen K and make it on to the run, then the Energy Lab is where your marathon can be won or lost. With only the moonlight and white lines on the road to guide me the atmosphere is eerie. The only sense I have that I am not alone is the glow sticks that fellow athletes wear. So dark it is that the glow sticks appear to be dancing, suspended in air. I cannot see my fellow athletes until they pass close by. The ungodly silence is occasionally broken by a race official on a motorbike approaching. On hearing the revving engine my heart skips a beat, as I fear I may be the next target. I have no idea how my progress is going, was I going to be the next casualty of this race?

I have been on the anvil for over 14 hours since 7am this morning. My body is beaten into a bloody mess, almost at the edge of submission. Every muscle in my being is in pain and I am exhausted beyond exhaustion. I have blisters on both feet. My armpits, groin and my butt are red raw from chaffing all day. My feverish skin looks like a cooked lobster and my neck, lower back and hips are stiff from the long bike ride. Putting one foot in front of the other has become an ordeal beyond anything I have ever encountered before, but I am not about to give in. My mind is still functioning and it is my mind that is in control of this beaten body.

I was born in the year of the Ox in the lunar calendar. According to the Chinese Zodiac, an Ox is a person with a strong will but also very stubborn and persistent. It is these traits that are now working to my advantage. Having come this far I was not about to roll over and admit defeat. Come what may, I will drag myself if needed to the finish line.

A little voice in my head keeps urging my body along, reminding me to focus and keep moving forward.

With no landmarks just barren lava fields and darkness the aid stations at 1.6km apart become my saviour. Illuminated by paraffin torches, their warm glow becomes a welcome beacon in the darkness, something for me to focus on. As I get closer the orange mirage grows brighter and I can hear tunes from a sound system breaking the silence. My heart skips a couple of beats and my step increases as I realize I am nearing salvation of energy bars, drinks, ice and water, fruits, cookies and medical aid all manned by volunteers with kind words of encouragement and big smiles that will spur me on my way for the next 1.6km. And that becomes my game, working from one beacon to the next until I find myself out of the hellish pit of torture that is the Energy Lab.

My spirit lifts as I leave the lava fields behind me. Now every step I take brings me one step closer to the finish line. Despite my mind being buoyed and excited by this news my body continues to argue and my physical condition only allows for at best a feeble jog. A mixture of walking and shuffling with my focus sternly on the bright lights of the Queen K up ahead as I slowly approach town. Each aid station I pass jerks me out of my slump as I am greeted with well wishes from volunteers. "Good job, you are looking great! Keep going!" I know these words of kindness are a bunch of bull crap lies. I know I look far from great. But they magically do the trick and I keep shuffling along.

I glance at my watch. It is 10:40pm and I am 6km from the finish line with 80 minutes to get there. The aid stations continue to be my saving grace where I receive not just necessary food and drink but much needed support from the volunteers telling me to not give up and get a move on. I am enjoying a welcome change of hot chicken soup and buns when I spy a cold can of Budweiser beer. Oh how I would love to taste that amber nectar. Snapping me out of my daydream a volunteer reads my thoughts and shouts out, "Don't you dare take that. You will be out of the race."

As I begin to move away from the aid station I hear the Michael Bolton song 'Going the Distance' playing from the sound system. The lyrics sound so sad and lonely, peaking my emotions. With tears welling in my eyes I stop to listen. But then another voice inside my head jolts me awake. "Hey man! You want to be an Ironman, you better get a move on!"

I keep assuring myself that the next hill is where I will see the finish. And then it becomes the next hill and the next until finally I can hear it. I can hear the razzmatazz of the finish line. I cannot see it but I can hear it. I can taste it.

The lights become brighter and Palani Drive is once again in sight. "I am coming home. I am going to be an Ironman." My spirit lifts and the hill that has tested me all day becomes less of an ordeal. Why did this hill hurt me so much before? I ask myself.

I take the final turn into Alii Drive and my dream is there laid out before me a mere 400 meters away. I can see it. Thundering music shakes the ground beneath me as I take my first steps on the finish line carpet and then from nowhere I find myself picking up speed in response to the cheers and shouts from the crowds of spectators lining the street.

And then I hear my name, those words I have waited for all day. "Participant 1479, Sze Mun Yee, 58 years old from Malaysia is coming in. He is going to make it." I make a dash for the last 200 meters, tears of joy rolling down my face, the pain has finally gone and I am flying, I am unstoppable. My emotions are suddenly in overdrive, all day long I have fought the demons, kept my emotions intact and now as I float down the hallowed carpet and cross the line under those heavenly arches all the excitement, sweetness of my victory, happiness and pride comes to a crescendo. And then, it is over. Everything stops and the flashbulbs from cameras bring me back down to ground with a solid bump.

"Sze Mun Yee, you are an Ironman!" Announced by the voice of Ironman, Mike Reilly. With 22 minutes and 39 seconds left – on my longest day I had made it.

At the finishing line of my first Hawaii Ironman.

18 | *This 'addiction' beats me up, yet I keep coming back for more…*

Celebrating my achievement with my wife, Sheila.

CHAPTER 2

From where I came...

Queen of Hearts, a tribute to 'Po Kee' Ah Ma

A mother's love for her child knows no bounds and my mother, Chew Po Kee exemplified this sentiment with absolute devotion to all her thirteen children.

Ah Ma as she was more fondly known came from a farming village across a river of Shantou on the eastern coast of Guangdong Province, China. She was one exceptional lady and I have nothing but great admiration for her gutsy character. I attribute much of my own mental strength and stubbornness today to my Ah Ma. At a young age I learnt to emulate the same resilience she practiced throughout her life.

I was born on June 19, 1937 in Malaysia into a lower middle class family. The eldest of thirteen, I have three brothers and nine sisters. Large families were very much the expected norm in those days. My early childhood was not luxurious but it was comfortable. The income from the family business, Joo Huat, was enough to put food on the table. Toys and games on the other hand were never available. They were alien to my siblings and I, and my father never indulged us with a toy of any sort. Instead, my brothers and sisters and I learned early on to improvise with discarded junk. We would collect bottle caps and empty cigarette boxes and use them as chips for games. We had never heard of bowling but we played a similar game using cigarette boxes. We would line up the empty boxes like ten pins and take turns to knock them down by sliding a flattened cigarette box towards the target. We would also race with bicycle wheel rims. Running along using a short stick in the rim to push it along. We would catch spiders in the undergrowth to fight with spiders other kids caught. And we would catch Siamese fighting fish from the streams for the same purpose. And marbles, we would play marbles. We did not have much but what we lacked in material possessions, toys and such we made up for with our imaginations to turn anything into a game. Those were my carefree days.

Ah Ma was a strong, tough no-nonsense lady who never had the luxury of taking it easy. She took care of her children and the household single-handedly all year round. Her thoughtfulness in caring for us had a compelling effect. I know that our welfare always took precedence over her interests, always. I never once saw Ah Ma eat before her children. She would always let us eat and select our food first, telling us not to waste anything. Once we had finished she would usually pick over the bones and finish the leftovers.

Despite being illiterate Ah Ma taught us well in life. She knew her children needed an education to secure a brighter future. Every day she walked me to school and would then return home and come back again to meet me from school in the midday heat. On the way home she would always try to give me a piggyback due to the heat, but I was always too proud to let her carry me.

Being the eldest child there were very few periods of time when Ah Ma was not with child. Her main role was procreation. Her life revolved adding a new 'recruit' to the family every twelve to eighteen months. We were always provided for despite the growing brood and despite Ah Ma carrying a new brother or sister for the most part of each year, she never slowed down, never complained. Not once.

In the mid 1940's when World War II was nearing its end my second sister Yee Kah Yam was brought into this world in extraordinary circumstances. Nothing fazed Ah Ma; even having to deliver her baby alone while Japanese bombers flew overhead.

Allied bombers had planned an air raid on Kuala Lumpur towards the end of World War II with the Malayan Railway central workshop one of the key targets in the raid. I clearly recall my entire family except for Ah Ma running for cover at the nearby bomb shelter. Ah Ma, in the advanced stage of her pregnancy with Kah Yam, was unable to make it to the safety of the shelter and stayed at home, taking cover under a simple wooden bed. When the assault ended, we returned home to find her lying in a pool of blood under her 'shelter'. She had gone into an early labour and delivered Kah Yam on her own. Survival and maternal instincts kicking in she had detached the umbilical cord by severing it with her teeth.

Kah Yam was the subject of another incident and display of Ah Ma's unconditional love and devotion a few years later. As a toddler learning to walk, my little sister was not yet steady on her chubby legs. Kah Yam was walking around the house and toddled out onto the open veranda. Our family was in the soap-making business and the veranda was where hot ashes were thrown to cool down for use in making soap. Unaware of the danger ahead, Kar Yam toddled out and took a tumble landing in the ashes severely burning and scarring both her legs for life.

As Kah Yam was recovering from the severe burns she was unable to walk and despite being force-fed painkillers at regular intervals my little sister would cry and scream in pain, stopping only when she had exhausted her little self. To help sooth Kah Yam, Ah Ma resorted to carrying Kah Yam day and night to help ease her suffering. Ah Ma was in the early stage of her pregnancy with my third sister and hardly ever had time to get any rest. I would often find Ah Ma asleep in a chair with Kar Yam in her arms.

Where was my father amidst all of this? If it were not for the continuing addition of brothers and sisters you might be fooled into thinking my mother was a single parent.

I cannot recall my father offering any help in the upbringing of all my siblings but I did have a father and his name was Yee Jun Kheng. My father hailed from a middle class family in Shantou (Swatow) in the coastal Eastern Guangdong. Ah Ma's and father's union was not the traditional happy marriage. It was an arranged marriage and far from 'happy'. My father left for Malaya soon after they were married and my mother, Ah Ma followed a year later.

Myself and my brothers and sisters never developed a strong bond with our father and our lack of respect and love for him extended to refusing to call him papa. Instead we followed our cousin's formal approach and addressed him as Poid Chek (meaning 8th Uncle). He was far from deserving of the name father.

Poid Chek had many bad habits and Ah Ma hated them all. My father was a bad drinker and gambler. He smoked and had a weak spot for attractive women.

When Ah Ma fell ill, Poid Chek would show little sympathy and failed to become for just once, the husband he should be and take care of his wife. After giving birth to one of my sisters Ah Ma came down with a very high fever and should have been hospitalised. Poid Chek did not send her to hospital or even take her to the clinic. Luckily for her children, Ah Ma was resilient and strong-willed. She never relied on anyone else let alone her husband and would get herself back to health with traditional Chinese remedies and medicines.

Poid Chek's personality was a striking contrast to that of the independence and strength of Ah Ma. They were like chalk and cheese. He was soft and sloppy. If Poid Chek ever showed the slightest sign of illness Lord help us. A bout of flu would send Poid Chek to bed for days moaning as if he was on his deathbed and he would become even more useless than normal.

During my childhood under British Colonial rule the English education system was prevalent in schools. Poid Chek was educated in China and spoke Mandarin. However when under the influence of alcohol the Malay and English phrases that he picked up working in Joo Huat would suddenly have him believe he was fluent in a language that combined colloquial Malay and English. It was perhaps the only entertainment he provided!

Family history from Malaysia to China

The journey of my mother and father comes from a large and complicated family tree.

Poid Chek's father, my grandfather, Yee had two wives. My grandmother was his first wife and together they had seven children. Aunt Tua Kor was the eldest, my father Poid Chek the youngest. I had five other uncles and two more uncles from grandfather Yee's second wife who were Poid Chek's half brothers.

The whole family lived as many Chinese families still do today, all under one roof. It was common for affluent men to take a second wife. She would live under the same roof and many times this would destroy the first marriage. Their house was a large three-storey home but after my grandfather's second marriage the family harmony (not surprisingly) fell apart and my grandmother fell out of favour with grandfather who had moved onto his new life with a new wife.

Grandfather Yee became engaged in a lengthy legal tussle with some business rivals and exhausted all financial resources through complicated family squabbles and business rivalries. He eventually won his legal battle but in the quest to save face and his dignity, his fortune was lost.

Uncle Tua Pek was disheartened at the family situation and, seeing no reason to stay in his homeland, chose to leave and seek greener pastures in Kuala Lumpur in the late 1920's. He found employment at the Malayan Railway central workshop and was promoted to foreman in the coach painting section. Always a thrifty fellow, Tua Pek saved his earnings and started Joo Huat, a small sundry shop selling provisions mainly to the railway workshop's workers and their families.

Almost a decade later, his brother (my father) Poid Chek came over from China to help Tua Pek run the shop. Ah Ma joined them a year later. My father was in his mid twenties and my mother just twenty.

Uncle Tua Pek and his wife Aunt Tua Sim had one son Michael Yew Yee Thye and an adopted daughter, Kar Hoon from Uncle Goh Pek. Kar Hoon's mother died during childbirth and in Chinese custom it was considered taboo for Goh Pek to keep his daughter and she was given away and adopted by Tua Pek while Goh Pek remained in Hong Kong. Tua Pek died in his early 40's from tuberculosis, after contracting the same virus from her husband Tua Sim passed not long after leaving their son and adopted daughter now in the care of my father. Through no fault of my cousins, their presence in the household increased the tension between my father and myself and my siblings.

Poid Chek took over the business and also the responsibility to raise his brothers' two children. My brothers and sisters and I started to feel neglected and there was a mutual feeling that Poid Chek, our 'father' was providing better for Michael and his sister than his own flesh and blood. I believe Poid Chek felt indebted to his late brother who had 'gifted' him the Joo Huat business and along with that came the responsibility of orphan Michael. It did little to help us understand the disparity. We just saw a 'father' who preferred our cousin.

Poid Chek hired two assistants and his half brother, See Pek (meaning 4th uncle in the Teochew dialect), to help out in the shop. In total there were twenty of us living under one small roof and our livelihood depended on the revenue generated from the goods we sold. Home was the shop, and it occupied two single storey unit terrace houses. Additional extensions were implemented over the course of time to accommodate all of us. There was just one bathroom and it was situated next to the kitchen.

The toilet was a small wooden cubicle about 10 meters from the shop. The toilet itself was basic at best – a concrete square with a hole in the middle where a bucket below held our excrement. The bucket was emptied once a week when the night 'soil' carriers were tasked with the job of going round the houses emptying the buckets. With 20 people under one roof, you can only begin to imagine how insufficient this service was. As the time neared for the weekly emptying, the combination of volume, humidity and tropical temperatures did not make trips to the toilet or surrounding area a pleasant experience.

There were just three rooms at the back of the shop. From the age of six when bedtime came round most of us children would set up a foldable canvas bed within the empty space. It was a hot and stuffy sleeping arrangement and the air was permeated with the unpleasant smell of mosquito coils emitting pungent smoke. It was not the healthiest of environment, and a proper rest was never possible, but we knew no different.

Life became more comfortable for my parents when we started to earn our own money. My first job was as a temporary teacher while waiting for my Form 5 results. I would give half of my wages to my parents. However, Ah Ma remained prudent and never allowed us to improve on our own standard of living.

Poid Chek was neither a perfect father nor a clever businessman but he was a man of integrity. He borrowed money for the business from many friends and always, eventually, settled his debts. He did not want to bring shame and disgrace on Joo Huat's reputation and go into the bad books of his creditors because of his own poor judgments. When the business collapsed, he did not default and run away. With the help from the allowances extended to him from my siblings and I he cleared his debt, but it took ten years to get there. I was in my thirties when Poid Chek was finally debt free.

Ah Ma lived to 76 and Poid Chek, 79. A row of double storey apartment houses was built after the landlord tore down the shop house. They purchased a first floor apartment with Kar Yam who was now married and stayed there until they passed away.

Shantou detour – An emotional wound

As the world recovered and healed from the end of World War II in 1945, life slowly regained normality as we knew it to be. As a young eight year old boy I was oblivious to any problem within our growing family; life was at times tough but we always had food on the table, Ah Ma always provided for us. The fact that brown rice once or twice a week was a luxury where in other households it was a daily staple was unknown to me. Fish and meat were rarely on the table and we relied on sweet potatoes and tapioca for our main fuel of carbohydrate. Vegetables came from a patch of empty land near the house where we grew and tended a vegetable garden. For Ah Ma those days must have been a struggle, to me it was normality – I knew no different.

In 1948, our excuse for a father, Poid Chek, sent my sister, Yee Ah Mooi and I away without explanation, away from Ah Ma and away from the 'comfortable' life we knew. We were both scared and confused and that day Poid Chek inflicted a deep emotional wound that remained unanswered. Ah Mooi was just ten and I a year older. Both innocent children in this act of rejection we had no choice but to abide by his wish to send us away to his native land in Shantou, China.

Until today I still cannot accept the fact that he sacrificed two of his eldest children for the sake of his opium-addict third brother, Sa Pek. Perhaps he thought we would get a better education and upbringing thousands of miles away in his motherland? And perhaps he thought his bachelor brother could benefit from raising two adopted kids? I know my dad had more children than he could handle but the way our departure was handled stung. Poid Chek did not consult with Ah Ma until after the decision was made, leaving her bitterly upset and unable to protest. Poid Chek was the master of the house in those days. There was no negotiating.

See Pek accompanied us to China with the hope of getting married in his native land. We travelled by train to Singapore before boarding a rusty cargo ship and tasted the hardships other migrants went through when embarking on similar journeys. There were no cabins on the ship, passengers slept and had their meals on the rows of wooden platforms in a section of the cargo hold.

We stopped at Haikou Port in Hainan and Hong Kong en route. It took more than a week to cover the journey. I remember it being very stuffy, hot and dirty and smelly from the less sea worthy passengers. It was most uncomfortable but we soon adjusted and I cannot recall if I was excited or scared, maybe a little of both? It was my first voyage by sea and despite the circumstances that prompted the trip as an 11-year-old boy I was naturally a little excited by the magnitude of the adventure.

This detour in the early stages of our teenage years was a learning curve that taught us both to be independent and to stand on our own two feet. We lived in Shantou for five long years. During this time it was Ah Ma's unconditional love, her kindness and tenderness and warmth that only a mother can provide that I missed most. Our immediate relatives were not the same. They had their own children and my sister and I were just an extra financial burden. I can't complain though. Even when I was flat broke I never approached my aunties for money. Once during the Lunar New Year I lost all the money I had in a card game with my cousins and friends. I had no money for the whole of the festive season. It was a valuable lesson at a very young age and I never have gambled again.

After my grandparents passed away, Sa Pek became the master of grandfather Yee's large three-storey house. As the eldest of the remaining siblings, Sa Pek assumed control of the Yee family estate. The newfound wealth and power went to his head and Sa Pek turned into a power hungry, opium addicted lord.

Residing in the same house, were Goh Sim, my fifth auntie and her stepson, Lak Sim my sixth auntie, her son and daughter and a servant.

It was completely normal for the men of the household not to work. With brothers working overseas, the household received a monthly remittance from our Hong Kong based Uncle Goh Pek and our father in Malaya. These monies were enough to cover household expenses including Sa Pek's twice daily fix of opium. Sa Pek became 'Master of the House' and in a way was performing his duties while his brothers worked overseas and remitted money back to support the household and his opium habit.

I did not think highly of Sa Pek because he did not pull his weight and did absolutely nothing to contribute to the family. But to be fair, he did have a silver lining. Despite his many faults he was a strict disciplinarian and did not compromise in instilling good behaviour. Good table manners for some reason were especially important to him. Dining was deemed an important family time and Sa Pek emphasized on this always being a time for peace and quiet. He wanted us to appreciate the hard-earned labour that had taken place to get food on the table. He did not like it when someone interrupted during these mealtimes. I remember that when dishes of food were served, we could only pick from sections nearest to us and he did not allow us to select our own preferred portions.

I was the second eldest of three boys in the house and admittedly a little bit of a rebel. As such I was frequently beaten by Sa Pek with his smoking pipe. Back then South East Asian countries were considered uncivilized and my Uncle would call me Sang Fan (an Aborigine) from the South Sea.

Studies took place in a missionary school and it was compulsory to attend church every Sunday. Despite bible classes and Sunday school that was enforced upon my young self I chose to be a free thinker. I have fond memories of my playtime every Sunday after church especially during the long hot summers.

Every Sunday my cousins Sze Keat, Sze Choon and I were required to attend Sunday school. As soon as school was out we would head straight to the seaside. The stern instructions from Sa Pek was to go out together and return together. Sze Keat is two years my senior and like myself shared a keen interest for outdoor adventure.

Sze Choon however, the youngest, was less adventurous. A timid and studious 'bookworm' type Sze Choon had a temper on him. Since he was scared of water we had to bribe him each week to come to the seaside. He would wait under the shade of a tree while my elder cousin and I enjoyed the beach and had our fun.

Despite our incentives and bribes to keep him on our good side Sze Choon spilled the beans on us on more than a few occasions. This was usually out of spite because we had kept him waiting a little too long in the heat of the day. As the leader of the pack I took the blame and dealt with the heavier punishment that was carried out by Sa Pek. Besides the usual caning I would have to go down on both knees and kneel for hours without food. My sister, Ah Mooi, God Bless Her, would sometimes sneak a bowl of plain porridge mixed with a little fermented bean sauce when Sa Pek had retired to his room for his opium fix.

The harsh punishment meted out did little to deter us. We continued to take our weekly outings to the beach after Sunday school and I eventually taught myself to swim.

Sze Choon never learnt to swim and he paid for this with his life years later when he took a plunge into the river one summer day while studying in university. He was just 18 years old. I was in shock but also struck by anger at Sze Choon when I learnt of the news. If only he had joined Sze Keat and I when we were playing in the sea on those Sundays he could have learnt to swim and may still be alive.

In 1949, one year after I had arrived in Shantou, the communists won the civil war against the Kuomintang government and China became a communist country. Life as I had become to know it changed from that day forward and I was not in favour of the change. Bible classes were replaced with ideology lessons, group meetings and self-criticism sessions.

My sister and I wanted to return to Malaya but we were not permitted to leave the country without a permit from the immigration office. Reasons for the rejection of the permit were unknown to us. Probably they were hoping that we would stay on and our families abroad would continue to support us and inject foreign funds into the country. We would beg, plead and sometimes cry with the authorities for permission to travel.

Ah Mooi and I took turns to go to the immigration office at regular intervals and pleaded with the officers in charge to allow us to leave. After two years of relentless visits and pleading we were both finally given the green light to leave China. In early March 1953 we departed Shantou by cargo ship and returned home to Kuala Lumpur via Singapore. I was 16 years old.

CHAPTER 3

The price of climbing the corporate ladder

Playing catch-up – the fast track education lane

The excitement surrounding our homecoming and the thrill to finally be reunited with my family in 1953 was short-lived. My cloud nine mood was brought down to earth with a bump and immediately replaced with a dreadful insecurity of my inability to communicate in the English language.

Under command of the British Colonials, English was the official language. While we were not free our struggle was one that I deemed a far better deal than what I had put up with under the autocratic communist regime in China.

On returning home my mind was focused on carving out a good future and working for the civil service was considered a safe, secure and promising career path. The downfall of this particular choice was that it came with the necessary requirement of reading and writing English. I was almost 16 when I returned home and my English proficiency was limited to the 26 letters of the alphabet so I was far from ready to enter the civil service workforce. I needed to earn the English Senior Cambridge certificate; I had a lot of ground to cover and almost eight years of catching up to do.

I could not follow the usual journey of starting from Standard One in renowned public schools as I was over 16 years of age and the public school system, while free, only accepted students of 'appropriate' school age for the class they were entering. Private school was my only option. The issue with the private school system was it cost us money we did not have and the quality of education was extremely poor. The advantage was they took anyone willing to pay the school fees. The disadvantage was many of the teachers of the lesser-known schools that I could afford were not even qualified and some teachers were even students themselves.

I had no choice but to make the best of the situation and work hard to earn the certificate.

In order to fast track my education I needed to switch schools each year as no school would allow you to skip years once you had enrolled. You could however enter another school at a higher year. Using my Chinese school certificate I conned entry into a new school each year and each time skipped a year. For the first six months I attended evening tuition classes starting from Standard One before I enrolled as a Standard Four pupil at a day school housed in a Sikh temple at Haji Salleh Road in Sentul. I then switched again and entered Standard Six at another substandard private school operating on the first floor of an Indian Muslim coffee shop the following year that was partitioned into three to four classrooms each with thirty plus desks. We were crammed and I stood out like a sore thumb being four to six years older than my classmates.

In my third year I was accepted as a Form Two student at another private school. I joined the C-class of the Commercial Institute located on the first floor of the Bata shoes shop at Batu Road (now known as Jalan Tunku Abdul Rahman). In the final three examinations I came first in my class and was promoted to A-Class for Form Three at the main school that occupied a large bungalow on top of a hill where the Kuala Lumpur Menara Tower is now situated. I emerged again as the top student in my class and also passed the Lower Certificate of Education.

I was on my way to achieving the required English Standard Cambridge Certificate and progressing at a fast rate but it did not come easy. While I was undertaking the certification, the family business began to face serious cash flow problems due to Poid Chek's failed ventures in rice milling and embroidery products. The lack of income also meant that Poid Chek could not finance my education. As I consistently earned top honours in the class, my class teacher from India recognised my desire to learn. He took pity on me and was kind enough to sponsor my school fees for the year.

I continued Form Four in the A-Class, but with no money to buy my own school books, I borrowed books from my friends in the B-Class. A-Class students were allowed to sit for qualifying tests, which were compulsory for all private school students hoping to move up to Form Five and take the senior Cambridge Certification Examination (my holy grail goal in all of this). I was first in class again for the final examination and also got through the qualifying tests at the year end.

In 1959 I was rated as the school's best hope to pass the Senior Cambridge Certification examination. I was by no means the smartest kid in class during my six years of education, what made the difference was I studied the hardest and had a specific goal driven by the need to survive later in life. My success in my final school had helped elevate their status to a reputable private education institution. As a reward the principal personally funded me a scholarship, excluding the expense for books. Still with no money to purchase the books, I continued to borrow from friends in the B-Class. Scholarships are almost unheard of among private schools and if it was not for the kind gesture of the principal and his recognition of my efforts, my life may have taken a completely different path.

I did not disappoint my school principal and passed the exam with a Grade Two certificate missing Grade One narrowly because I failed to earn a credit in English. I sat for a supplementary exam and secured a credit for the subject the following year.

It took me six years to get my Senior Cambridge Certificate, a process that is normally attained over eleven years. My success in academic studies was not through a luxury of solely focusing on preparing for my examinations. As soon as I returned home each day I was required to help out in the shop for a few hours each day. When I was at school I had to ensure I studied hard as I knew there would be no time for studies at home.

My struggle to get a proper education and the learning experience that came with it had a significant impact on my young adult life. After six years I left school a better man because of the inevitable circumstances forced upon me to walk the extra miles and travel the education path less taken.

It was my first triumph, pulling off feats that initially appeared to be beyond reach and also to mark the start of prevailing over many more tricky challenges that lay ahead.

I am not gifted with any particular talent, but what I have accomplished I have done so with an iron will to carry out the seemingly impossible against odds. Success can be gauged on many different levels but it can only be achieved by sheer hard work and determination. There are no gifts, no silver platter and no free ride.

Joining the workforce – learning all the way

Teaching was my first job but I knew that I was not destined to seriously pursue a career as a qualified educator. I wanted more.

It was not by choice when I started to give private tuition classes a week after completing final examinations. A teaching credential was not required for many private schools and despite the wages being a pittance they helped alleviate the immediate financial problem my family was facing. I entered into it knowing that it would be short term only. Poid Chek was in serious financial difficulties and I was obliged to do all I could to supplement the family income. It was a temporary fix to help out my family so when the new academic term began I took up the offer and taught at a private school in Pudu Road, Kuala Lumpur.

Eight months passed and an opportunity presented itself with a British company specialising in industrial and medical gases at Chan Sow Lin Road in Kuala Lumpur. My teaching days were over and I was able to move on to take up a position on the bottom rung of the ladder as an order clerk.

My immediate superior was a sales clerk and we reported directly to an Englishman by the name of B.A.R. Smith. Both of us handled the entire company's sales enquiries that came in via mail, telephone and over the counter. We also sorted out orders secured by another two sales reps.

The sales clerk left six weeks after I arrived before I had any real time to settle in. His replacement lasted less than three weeks, walking out one day after an argument with Smith. Smith had terrible people skills and an old colonial attitude that did not sit well with many locals. For these reasons he was transferred the following month back to Singapore and in his place arrived another Englishman, Tony Goodwin. Tony was tasked with reorganizing operations in Kuala Lumpur. A capable engineer by the name of Yeow Koon Wee also came over to assist him.

I had an opportunity to grow and despite my lack of training I was immediately thrown into running the sales office single handedly. Even though I was not familiar with the company's core business in industrial and medical gases, Yeow encouraged me to prove myself because he saw an opportunity for me to advance in my career.

To get up to speed with the product I learnt to be resourceful and read through the company's backdated correspondence files and product catalogues. I also quickly learnt that by 'treating' the salesman encouraged them to share their knowledge on company products thus increasing my knowledge.

The days were long and I extended my hours without any incentive by working until 8pm every day to complete my tasks and cover for the vacant sales clerk. Lunch was 15 minutes, sometimes 20 if I was lucky after which I headed to the company's welding school to learn gas and arc welding. I worked six days a week and also most Sundays for half a day. During this time I never received any extra money or incentive for all the extra hours I incurred. This role continued for almost three months and through that time I managed to keep the company's sales office afloat. I definitely was not expected to shoulder the extra work; I basically just took it upon myself. The set-up was in a mess. My conscience would not allow me to leave without clearing my desk and that of the vacant sales clerk each day. I held onto the thought that Yeow told me that with the right attitude there was an opportunity to learn and grow and progress. Yeow honoured those very words with my first advancement not long after.

When the company could not hire a replacement sales clerk after three months of searching the manager offered me the position. This was my first step up a very long ladder.

Two years later I was selected to go to Australia for a three month specialized product training conducted by the company's Australian associates in Sydney and Melbourne. I returned home and took up position as specialist sales representative for paint spray products in Malaysia and Singapore.

Six years later in 1970 I was seconded to the Australian associates as regional sales manager responsible for the South East Asian market division including Hong Kong and Taiwan. I was away six months of the year working overseas and I wore a different hat as the product manager for Malaysia and Singapore every time I returned back home. Although I had a hectic working life and schedule as I moved up the corporate ladder my life improved. Overseas travel allowances and a better pay allowed me to save up and buy my first single storey terrace house.

I still wanted more. I wanted to be the boss of my own fate and in 1976, six and a half years after holding the position of 'Regional Sales Manager' I left my job and started up Panweld Sdn Bhd (Co Ltd) in partnership with a Singaporean and two other Malaysians. We commenced operations on April Fool's Day 1976 and took over the Devilbliss spray paint equipment agency and distributorship from the USA.

One year short of turning 40, I sold my house to fund the company and it was the beginning of another chapter of a new struggle of my life.

It was a totally different ball game operating my own business because it was so much more complex than other jobs. I went through ups and downs tackling new challenges and clearing unknown obstacles.

Regardless of the outcome, I always came out richer in knowledge and stronger in confidence after overcoming such hurdles along the way.

Unavoidable circumstances denied me a chance to attain a tertiary education but I felt I compensated with priceless experiences learning on the job throughout my working life.

A life changing transition – the wake up call

It was a normal stopover to pick up a roast duck takeaway dinner at Sea Park in Petaling Jaya.

One late evening in 1985, the unusual facade of a new medical clinic located on the same row of shop houses as my favourite roast duck takeaway turned out to be a significant turning point in my life. I had stopped to admire the stylish decoration and interior more fitting to that of a cosy hotel lounge rather than a clinic when a young Indian doctor came over and greeted me. I praised him for the modern, inviting design of his clinic.

We exchanged name cards and after a friendly conversation he invited me to visit his consultation room for a check up.

At 48 years of age I had my first medical examination, I had no idea, no idea whatsoever about my current state of my health or lack of. The moment of truth appeared when he ran through the results of my blood and electrocardiogram (ECG) tests the following week. Everything was high including my blood sugar levels, blood pressure, cholesterol and uric acid.

Looking at my beer belly and the spares tires protruding over my pants, I admit I was not in my best physical condition. It was a long overdue albeit unexpected wake-up call.

The doctor advised me to shape up and get fit if I had any hope of living beyond 60. That same year, (at the recommendation of a colleague from my company's overseas office) I was talked into having my future read by a well-known Indian palm reader. He predicted the almost identical fate and indicated that my lifeline would currently end at 67.

A panic alarm had been triggered. The cumulative consequences of chasing after wealth at the expense of my health for the past 20 years had resulted in a weak, unhealthy body. I decided to make some positive changes to my lifestyle and get back in shape.

Exercising suddenly took precedence over my previous after-work pastime of Happy Hour at local drinking holes. I reduced Happy Hour sessions to once a week and replaced them with three to four exercise sessions.

After eight months of weight training there were visible signs of major muscle groups firming up and making an appearance after years and years of being hidden beneath layers of fat. The one remaining stubborn layer was my potbelly. Standing at only 5ft 2", despite my best efforts, every extra remaining kg seemed to be hanging around my waistline.

In an effort to reduce the belly I started to include jogging, as part of my daily workout as a gym buddy assured me this was the most effective way to trim down belly size!

Conveniently for me there was a lake which is part of the Subang Ria Park behind the hotel within which my gym was located. One lap around the lake is about 1.1km. On my first attempt I ran two rounds with a little walking in-between.

I found great joy in doing this new activity and included two sessions of jogging to complement another two sessions of weight lifting each week. I also started to jog one loop as a warm-up before each weight lifting session at the gym. Gradually my endurance improved and after 10 weeks I was able to complete eight laps totalling 8.8km non-stop around the lake.

I was beginning to look a lot like my former slimmer self. A person that I thought had been lost forever when I started to pile on the pounds in my early 40's. Feeling upbeat, with renewed energy and a new fit body my life was starting again at 50! To celebrate my reclaimed health I took part in my first ever road running event – The Star PJ Half Marathon on August 23, 1987.

Up until now my running had not exceeded 8.8km. Taking the first of many brave new steps forward I would be running 21.1km – more than double my longest training run. Race day arrived and I reached the 12km mark without stopping (with the exception of slowing down through aid stations). From 12km onwards it became a jog-walk-rhythm for the next 3km before my lack of distance running delivered a new pain I had not yet encountered – muscle fatigue and blisters!

I was wearing oversized shoes; the combination of this and my wet socks had caused blisters on my feet, causing me to stop. I sat down on the kerb at the side of the road and took off my oversize shoes and wet socks to try and give my poor feet some relief before I carried on.

I was a little disappointed to retire at this point but I found comfort in the fact that I had reached 15km, 6km further than I had ever ran in my life prior to that. As I was pondering my next move with my mindset thinking that I had done enough for my first try, a plump lady jogged past me. She did not demonstrate the perfect running form and looked far from the perfect 'athlete' but she was making progress. She was moving forward and making better progress than I.

As I watched her pass by I saw her rear end wobble with every step she took. It didn't make me laugh, far from it; it inspired me to put my shoes back on and stop whining.

I did not feel the fatigue and pain that forced me to stop and take a breather earlier. My irritated inner voice also encouraged me to get my own arse moving. I felt disturbed and inferior noticing a plus size lady taking part in the race, running past me towards the finish line. I was no longer overweight. How could this be?

My ego was seriously ignited and I was not going to let this wobbly lady beat me. I would not take this lying down! It was a futile attempt to give chase and get closer to the lady but it was my anger that drove me forward. Besides the pain from the blisters and blue-black toenails, my legs were getting heavier towards the closing stages of the race.

After getting suckered into enduring the final 6km, I swore it would be my first and last half marathon. In the end I managed to drag my weary body to cross the finish line in 2hr 23min 42sec and went home with a finisher's medal along with a certificate. This was my first taste of a personal sporting achievement.

For the next nine months I was on a roll, showing up and completing half marathons in Kuantan, Desaru and Ipoh. On April 2, 1989 I completed my first full marathon in a time of 4hr 54min 50sec at the Kuala Lumpur international marathon. I clocked an improved 4hr 47min 51sec four months later at the Penang International Marathon.

My newfound sporting life continued to trump my former 'Happy-Hour' self. I was becoming addicted to this new healthy lifestyle, caught in its grip and constantly looking for new sporting challenges to put myself through. In between the two full marathons I also took part in my first multi-sport race comprising of a 1.5km swim, 42km bike and 10km run at the Port Dickson International Triathlon. A sport still in its infancy, my multi-sport début in the 50 plus age group rewarded me a very proud second place in a time of 3 hours 22 minutes and 45 seconds.

CHAPTER 4

Life changes at 50

A humbling experience – three little girls and a foolish me

In just three races over the past six months I had reduced my half marathon time by more than 12 minutes. With my confidence high I was certain that another personal best would be my reward as I readied myself for the Ipoh Half Marathon on May 29, 1988.

Despite my running improvements I knew I was still lagging behind many others in the 50 and over age group. It was in part my own doing, the fact that I was playing catch up this late in the day. Starting from scratch after a long hibernation and couch potato lifestyle for the best part of twenty-five years, I took consolation that at least now I was on the right track to a better lifestyle.

I knew I had already come a long way. Overcoming my first painful half marathon just six months earlier, I had cursed and swore that it would be my first and last 'taste' of this new lifestyle when I was forced to stop at the kerb to nurse my feet only to then drag myself the final 6km and cross the finish line. After crossing my first finish line the pain subsided and my spirits lifted. My fire reignited and I was soon in search of the next event.

Three months later in Kuantan I ran almost eight minutes faster clocking 2:16:08 and then four months later on undulating terrain I shaved more time off awarding myself a new personal best at the Desaru Half Marathon with a time of 2:11:32.

With three half marathons under my belt, you can imagine how powerful and unstoppable this new runner, who thought he was now an expert felt. I was now appropriately kitted out in the latest running attire and actually looked the part rather than standing out as a newbie. With the correct shoes and a relatively flat course ahead of me I was aiming for a sub 2-hour half marathon. Nothing could go wrong. Or so I thought!

Like all 'expert' runners, I had a plan. And my plan was to follow an average pace between 5:20 and 5:40 minute per kilometre that would allow me to dip below the two hour mark.

Everything was going to plan and I crossed the 10km point comfortably in 55 minutes. The real drama of my race began to unfold after I took a drink at a water station and let my focus and attention drift to a loud chattering in Tamil.

I looked over at the chatter and saw three little Indian girls not too far ahead. They were upper primary school, dressed in their white shirts and dark blue dress school uniform. I was taken aback at these skinny lasses running barefoot, and more to the point, running in front of me, so I stepped up my pace to catch them.

From close up the girls were even skinnier than I first thought, their tiny bodies gave the impression that they were suffering from malnutrition. Looking at their extremely thin physique I tried to figure out their high energy level. How were they running faster than me? I really was in disbelief. I looked the part. I was wearing 'the' shoes and looked stronger. So how were they running ahead of me and so easily?

In my limited command of Tamil-Malay I asked them; "Yapudee tangachi, enna sapadee elek?" English translation, "Girls, why are you running without shoes?"

One of them looked back at me and saw that I was running behind them, trying in earnest to keep up. She replied in Tamil something that I could not understand and from her annoyed expression I assumed it sounded something like, "mind your own business old man!"

I continued stalking them for a while and I had to increase my pace above my comfort level, just a little, to keep up with them.

It was then that I remembered a cheeky Indian song that I could hum the starting verse from. The original lines dedicated to a well-known retired local Indian politician were "Aiyo Samy, Avodee Samy, Aiyo Samy…" I changed the lyrics to "Aiyo tangachi, Avodee tangachi, Aiyo yo tangachi, Sapdee elek Aiyo yo? Which in English translated to – "Aiyo yo, girls you are running without shoes!"

I honestly was just trying to be friendly but it fell flat and the trio did not find my 'song' very friendly or amusing. Offended by my impractical

* Hello young girls! Why no shoes?

joke they turned up a gear and kicked harder in their ploy to lose me.

The stubborn egotistical old man that I am refused to give up. I had long ago stopped running 'my race' (the number one rule of running) and kept trailing behind them, my breathing becoming more and more laboured as the minutes ticked on. But I was not ready to accept defeat just yet and stuck with them until the next water station.

It must have been the lack of oxygen going to my brain because instead of bowing out, admitting defeat and dropping back to my own attainable pace I made a bigger blunder by trying to be funny again.

This time I engaged my mouth into gear without thinking of the dreadful consequences. In Malay, I told the volunteers at the aid station, "Bagi tangachi susu lembu!" (give cow's milk to the girls). I was insinuating that the little girls needed milk to grow and go faster (not that they needed it at all) and it served to add more spark to the girls.

"Old man go suck your mother's milk," they shouted at me. As if I was the one that needed the extra boost and help to keep up with them.

That was the last straw and stirred up a hornet's nest with the young trio. They turned at me, gave me an ugly look and then one of them shouted in Tamil which I did not understand but knew it was far from a compliment to this rude man (me).

When they took off again the girls did not show any signs of slowing down. They stopped chattering to increase their tempo and their breathing became more laboured under their increased speed. I had to slog to stay within reach of them until the pain became unbearable and the pace impossible to maintain.

My pride had finally got the best of me and paying the price, I stopped and pretended to bend down and tie my shoelaces hoping to back out of the duel without them noticing. Alas, my trick did not work. On noticing I was no longer huffing and puffing in their shadow one of the girls came back and shouted at me in full view of runners coming from behind. She gave me a taste of my own medicine shouting in full earshot of every runner around, "Aiya, pergi sedut susu Ah Ma!" (Go suck YOUR mother's milk!)

With my tank on empty I could do nothing in response to her insult. All I could muster was a meek smile and laugh at my own folly as I told her: "Por-por, tangachi" (Go-go girl) seeking for her to leave me alone and part on good terms.

I slowly dragged my weary spent humiliated body to the next aid station through a mixture of walking and slow jogging. I only have myself to blame myself for my own cockiness and foolishness getting sucked into the self-inflicted ego trap.

My dream for a sub two hour finish was derailed and in tatters. I ended up with a new personal best finishing in 2:05:52. But it was not the sub two hours I knew I had in me. The three little Indian girls did

* go suck your mother's milk old man.

not only offer me a very humbling experience but they also guided me through a valuable lesson to always, beyond all else, remain level-headed and race YOUR race.

Thank you 'Tangachi' for the loud and clear reminder of not to underestimate and undermine others irrespective of their age, gender and appearance. It also taught me to know my limits and not to get distracted from sticking to my own game plan by following my own pace to achieve my own personal goal.

Footnote: I did eventually go sub two hours in a half marathon when I least expected it. It was not official and was after a night of beers and fish head curry with members of the Triathlon Association of Malaysia. I rolled up to the start line at 5:30am with less that four hours sleep and surprised myself with a sub 2 hours 21km.

Accidental Initiation – Back on the saddle with the tricky pedals

Early in 1989 during a day trip to Port Dickson I saw a large banner promoting Port Dickson International Triathlon in front of the Port Dickson Yacht Club. Curious at what this 'International Triathlon' was all about, I decided to seek out further details inside.

At the end of my visit, I discovered the rudimentary principles of a triathlon. Participants had to take on a three-discipline race of Swim, Bike and Run. This particular race required participants to swim 1.5km, bike 42km and run 10km. Having no knowledge of the sport other than what I had just learnt I did the only thing that made sense to me and signed up. I knew running was no issue and swimming I could handle but I was currently without a bike and had not been on one for many years. It was February and the event was early June. I had three months to get back in the saddle!

Before signing up for PD triathlon my longest swimming session to date had been ten laps in a 25-metre pool once a week. I increased my distance to twenty laps and went on to put in between 1000m and 1500m in each session twice weekly. I was not concerned with speed in the pool. My goal was to emerge from the water and get to T1 and start cycling.

I already had several half marathons under my belt and was in the midst of training for my first full marathon. With the confidence of knowing I could tackle long distances, the running segment was no concern to me at all.

I was concerned however at the cycling portion of the race. It had been twenty-eight years since I was last on a bicycle and it was going to be a combined test of patience and recalling the skill needed to propel two wheels forward for a distance of 42km.

My cycling misadventures started with a 12-year-old rusty Raleigh road bike that belonged to my nephew. I wisely (so I thought) took the bicycle to be serviced at a shop near my office in Subang Jaya. My first attempt to get on turned into an embarrassing disaster right in front of the shop; why I couldn't have waited to try it out back at home I will never know!

In theory I did everything correctly. I tried to mount the bicycle by placing my left foot on the left pedal and got it moving before swinging my right leg over the rear wheel. Sounds like the perfect approach right? Well, it would have been had it not been for my baggy shorts that caught on the saddle as I attempted to hoist my leg over the top tube and down I went.

The bicycle mechanic came out and offered a safer approach to getting butt in saddle, but not before he had enjoyed a good laugh at my expense. Despite the new advice I could not do as instructed because the bike was so oversized for my short legs that I couldn't even touch the ground.

I had to go in between the top tube to maintain my balance and for both legs to stay in contact with the ground before I could get the bike moving. I also had to complete each rotation with my butt swaying from side to side due to the over-extended pedalling motion. It was definitely not a proper cycling technique but it was the best solution to handle such a cumbersome bike. I was not prepared to invest in anything more suitable until I was sure that I would like this new sport and continue to train and pursue triathlon.

Fifteen minutes into my first ride around the shop houses I was beginning to feel more comfortable and found the courage to change gears using the gear shifter located on the down tube.

And then just as my confidence was growing I made the error of back pedalling down a hill, causing the chain to drop. I panicked by jamming both brakes on and in the process caused the rear wheel to lift up and flip over. As a result of the forward force from the hard braking and stopping the front wheel so suddenly catapulted me over the top landing in the middle of the road providing an unexpected mid Saturday afternoon entertainment for the shoppers and passers-by.

I headed to a nearby furniture shop to recover from the shock of my unexpected dismount. The owner who was an old acquaintance offered me a drink and questioned my intentions in having a go at this riding a bicycle lark.

He suggested that 'at my age' I should instead be swinging golf clubs at a more leisurely pace around the golf course. I did not feel immediate pain and it was only when I examined my injuries that I found I had dislocated my thumb and had some colourful bruises on my right palm and knee. Despite the advice and injuries, his words fell of deaf ears.

My family also told me to forget about triathlon and again introduced the idea of golf as a more suitable pastime for a 'man of my age'. They felt that I was too old to start taking part in such a demanding sport from scratch.

Despite my initial setback I was not giving in. Born in the year of the Ox I am by nature as stubborn as they come, and any setbacks (minor or major) only served to fuel my ambition further.

I was however not totally blind to my family's concerns. And to appease them and soften any further mishaps I invested in some elbow pads, knee pads, gloves and helmet to assure my family and myself that I would be safe and sound in the future.

I also decided to look for a safer place to practice riding the bicycle and the Subang Jaya Ria jogging track that I knew so well seemed to be the perfect choice away from the road and traffic. My first attempt there however turned out to be my first and last as the security staff reprimanded me for creating such a hazard to other people using the track.

So I shifted to another location and cycled around the SS3 residential area in Petaling Jaya. A relatively peaceful middle class neighbourhood I still had to face my fair share of obstacles and be especially vigilant and on the lookout for unpredictable vehicles approaching from the side roads. I survived a few close calls and escaped with minor falls because I could not get on my feet quick enough to balance after avoiding the accident by pressing hard on the brakes.

Just when I thought this cycling malarkey could get no harder a new hazard confronted me. A group of mischievous children riding BMX's took it upon themselves to make nasty remarks and tease me whilst I rode around SS3. They would shout 'Ah Pek' (Old Man). Respect for a 52-year-old man was nowhere to be found.

On noticing my baggy attire, long socks, padded elbows, knees, helmet and gloves, the bullies nicknamed me a Mutant Ninja Turtle. It really didn't help that the most significant resemblance was the oversized

helmet that took on the appearance of a turtle shell on my head!

Undeterred, I could put up with the taunts and name-calling. It was when they started to race and play dangerous tricks on me that I became concerned for my safety. They would cut, skid and stop suddenly in front of me as part of their intimidating antics. I fell on a few occasions while they continued having fun pulling off their stunts. I did not sustain any further injuries because now I was protected to the hilt – a la Mutant Ninja Turtle. Sadly, however, I did not have Ninja Turtle powers to deal with my juvenile pests. And so my annoyance continued to grow and eventually they won. I was fed up of the tricks and remarks and those pests drove me out of my own neighbourhood and I had to find a new place to practice. So much for respecting your elders!

I still needed to get the riding discipline honed so I decided to travel to Port Dickson for weekend cycling sessions. I completed one session in the afternoon upon my arrival on the Saturday and covered the entire cycling distance for the triathlon on Sunday before returning home. It turned out to be a blessing in disguise because it served as a good advantageous preparation to be familiar with the actual cycling course for the race day.

Swim, Bike, Run – My first Triathlon

On Sunday 4th June, 1989 at 6:00am I pushed my bicycle into the parking lot of the Port Dickson Yacht Club that formed the transition area of the inaugural Port Dickson International Triathlon. My arrival attracted a fair bit of attention among other athletes. It was not that I was a VIP nor a celebrity but my general appearance and 'tri-gear' was received with what I can only explain as shock and awe.

I was equipped as I had been throughout my training, complete with elbow and kneepads, gloves and the oversized Giro helmet that came covered with a fabric of red and white stripes. Resting on the bridge of my nose was a pair of cheap sunglasses brought from the local pasar malam (night market). My running shoes were too large and I wore long white socks (long before compression became trendy). The socks reached over my knees on my short legs. Paired with long baggy shorts, my legs were completely covered. The official race singlet was way oversized and hung like a tent on my small frame. In addition to 'my' regular necessities I also brought along a large towel, a plastic pail (to wash my feet after the swim) and a low plastic stool to sit on while washing my feet. My bike was a 12-year-old Raleigh that I had borrowed from my nephew and was three sizes too big.

The race attracted two hundred plus participants and among them was a busload of athletes from Singapore. Three of the Singaporeans particularly stood out. Whilst I stood out for my unorthodox attire and equipment, the three Singaporeans in their mid 20's and early 30's stood out for all the right reasons. They had the triathlon build and tan and were equipped with the latest and greatest triathlon bikes and gear not yet available in Malaysia. Sadly they were also noisy and rather cocky, behaving like wanna-be pros. They took one look at me and exclaimed, "Yak, where is this old man from?" Perhaps they thought I was a clown

the Clown

engaged for a sideshow to spice up the event. I was so embarrassed by their stares and presence that I hurriedly left the transition area to have my body marked and then headed alone to the beach. Never have I been made to feel so small and out of place in my entire life.

Though I was one of the last few athletes to enter the water of the swim start I made steady progress and completed the swim ahead of a fair few athletes. But the time I had made up on the swim was lost as it took me forever to get through transition. Having decided prior to the race that I would wash my feet, dry my feet, put on all my protective gears (knee pads, elbow pads etc) and change from swimming trunks to jogging shorts, time was ticking away. Then the chord of my shorts snapped and caused me a few extra minutes to fix it.

Finally! I was on my way until one hundred metres into my ride I had to dismount as the front wheel was rubbing against the fork. I wheeled the bike back into transition and sought the assistance of technical support to fix it. More time was lost but I was in no hurry as my main goal was to see if I could complete the race.

Despite time lost messing about in transition and fixing my bike I was not the last athlete to complete the 42km and my heart lifted on learning this fact. For although my goal was to simply finish, no one wants to be last, especially not this old man.

The run leg was problem free, although I had to walk a bit between the aid stations. The issue was, I had no clue about the correct 'bike to run' routine and ran out of transition wearing my bike helmet complete with protective gear. No one told me otherwise and I figured I had already lost so much time already that I did not want to waste even more.

I must have looked quite the 'special attraction' as I sensed a fair few stares from both spectators and other athletes. It did little to bother me and I crossed the line in a time of 3:22:04. Very tired but immensely proud and satisfied that I had completed this new challenge.

With completion of my first triathlon under my belt there was an even bigger reward in store. Remember the old saying – 'He who laughs first, laughs last?' Well, I came across the cocky Singaporeans who did nothing but belittle me while setting up in transition. After the race two of them were laid out on stretchers. I did not know if they had completed

My last Laugh

the race or not, but seeing them on IV drips made my day. I felt very proud and made sure that they noticed me standing there, my finisher medal hanging around my neck.

Unbeknown to me at the time I had come in second out of eight in my age group. Had I known it then I would have made sure they noticed my trophy as well!

A week later my second place trophy, a pewter cup came in the post, I was so proud. I had found a new love. I went ahead and purchased my first road bike for RM760. Still one size too large it was all that was available for the money. I also purchased the correct size helmet, bike shoes complete with cleats (they took some getting used to) and appropriate cycling attire.

The foot that carried me across the finish line began the first step in a life long pursuit of my new obsession – the multi-disciplined sport of triathlon. My life had changed, it entered a new era filled with adventure, excitement, fun, new experiences and knowledge and lots of satisfaction. Albeit not without much blood, sweat and tears of some misadventures, mishaps, disappointment, sacrifice, but I've always been a glass half-full kinda guy.

Unpredictable tides – Kapas to Marang Swimathon

Swimming was the shortest discipline in my newfound love, triathlon. Wanting to challenge myself further in the water I decided to check off a bucket list item and sign up for a long distance swimming event.

The event in my sights was the inaugural Kapas to Marang swimathon. With about eighty swimmers from various clubs around the country in attendance, the majority were youngsters and I was considered the 'grandfather' at the ripe old age of 58. I was in the oldest age group of 35 and above. Senior veterans were an unknown age group back then!

When signing up for my new swim challenge I was also in the midst of training for my debut appearance at the Ironman Triathlon World Championships in Hawaii. The swim distance in Ironman is 3.8km so I figured this early swim test four months out from the October Ironman would be a great challenge and training day.

Getting myself in shape for both events was more a mental than physical test. I persevered with the boring monotony and mentally exhausting exercise of chalking 300 lap swimming sessions in an awkward 24m swimming pool at Fraser Towers condominium in Gasing Heights, PJ. My stroke of choice was breaststroke. It was by far the slower choice but I was far more at ease with this stroke for open water swimming.

The distance from Kapas to Marang as the crow flies measures 6.5km. Throw in unpredictable elements such as undercurrents and receding tides and your guess is as good as mine at predicting the average variable distance each swimmer would have to cover before reaching land.

A swimming coach from another state was hired to assist the rather 'green' inexperienced local hosts to run the event that was part of a water sports festival in Terengganu.

On the eve of the race during briefing, we learnt that we had three hours to swim to Marang after the 7am flag off. We were warned that the strong spring tide would start to recede at 10am and so after the three hour cut off, swimmers still in the water would be fished out as a safety precaution and classified as DNF (did not finish). The officials could not provide any forecast for the conditions so we were left to 'figure it out' on the actual day and hope for the best conditions possible. It was 1995 and the ease of information through a simple weather 'App' on your mobile phone was yet to be discovered.

The swim coach suggested using three white bungalows on the horizon behind the finishing arch at Marang as a sighting landmark. Over on Kapas island these bungalows and a large white balloon at the finish were barely visible and I knew once in the water should a large swell occur, there would be no possibility of sighting them.

As if hearing my concerns, the official assured us that the lead boat would be guiding all swimmers and that we could count on the lifeguards. Okay, nothing to worry about then, I told myself.

Race day dawned and more than an hour of crucial swimming time was lost we were kept waiting for the arrival of a 'VVIP' to officially start the event. This is an occurrence that to this day still goes on, yet no event gets flagged off without a so-called VVIP.

Before I could get into my swimming rhythm, my goggles started fogging up. I could not see clearly and my vision was limited to the surface of the water. The rising sun's rays further compounded my misery.

It seems I had contaminated my goggles when I applied sun block on another participant's back. A lifeguard came to check on me and I hung onto the Jet Ski while clearing my goggles before continuing. By then the lead boat had long gone and disappeared with the group of elite swimmers trailing behind it.

For the slow swimmers we stayed inside a safety lane with three boats forming two lines on each side. I took it for granted that swimming inside these parameters would be safe and so did little to confirm my own position relying completely on the group.

I recall the current was flowing left to right, as this happened we made adjustments to swim left and get back into lane when we found ourselves drifting outside the right lane. The boats were also correcting their positions under the same circumstances. We did the same manoeuvre a few times before I got tired of the back and forth and decided to leave the formation and swim on my own heading diagonally to the left against the current. My progress was slow but I felt in control of my own destiny with the three white houses staying on my left slowly becoming more visible with each stroke. Nobody was around me and I could hear only the noise of the Jet Ski machines occasionally speeding past from a distance.

I do not know how much time had passed but the next time I lifted my head up to confirm my position I was shocked to see the three white houses on my right. From the previous strategy of swimming diagonally to the left I changed direction and headed straight back towards the three white houses but I still could not see the white balloon and the finishing arch.

Luckily, the sea was surprisingly calm and I got into a consistent momentum, making encouraging progress mid-way through the race. As the image of the three houses grew bigger I started to visualize about the significance of my achievement on crossing the finishing line.

Suddenly I heard the revving of a Jet Ski shake me from my calm focus. "Swim to your right, swim to your right," shouted the lifeguard.

Once again, another check on my position revealed that I was very far left of the three white houses. They now appeared to be smaller compared to my previous sighting a short while ago. What on earth was going on?

I had been caught off guard again with the ever-changing current from right to left and had to change again and start swimming diagonally to the right.

It was the beginning of a very tough challenge. As a novice swimmer the intimidating receding tide was about to pose a serious danger. It was a scary experience to say the least and felt at times like I was swimming on the spot. Some younger participants who were undeniably faster and stronger gave up due to confusion and fatigue. I, however, was damned if I was going to give up after coming this far. I had already been in the water for two hours and I was determined to continue and push forward to get closer to the shoreline even if it was not the exact finishing area. Safety and survival and finishing this damn thing were now my order of priority!

I swam for my life and headed straight for dry land knowing that I could go under if the rescue team failed to reach me in a time of distress. After fighting the tide head on for an unknown amount of time my effort was not in vain and I was rewarded with the sight of the big balloon at the finishing line far long on my right.

As I got nearer to shore the conditions became more forgiving and I had to swim a short distance parallel to the beach to align my position and get to the finishing arch. Although I could hardly stand on my feet after completing the course in 2:57 for fourth spot in my age group I was over the moon with my courage to prevail over my adversities in my first attempt at a long distance swim.

After my initial experience at Kapas I returned three times and each year encountered a new set of difficult circumstances. Despite choppy seas and jellyfish stings I improved on my time and registered a personal best of 2:34 in my fourth-consecutive attempt at age 61. Not bad for an old 'grandfather!'

It was a testament in proving my belief that improving with age is possible if you do it the right way.

CHAPTER 5

You are never too old to take on new challenges

Improving with age

"Age is catching up with you." "You have already proven yourself." "You should take it easy." "Go and play golf." "Go for morning walks." It seems everyone had 'advice' for me when year after year I failed to break the 15-hour barrier in an Ironman race. While I appreciated family and friends' concerns, the words as usual fell on very deaf ears.

Since my very first Ironman race in 1995, Kona, Hawaii where I chalked up a time of 16:37:21 my performance has plateaued, always hovering around the 15-hour mark. I did 15:06 twice and 15:05 once. And then I peaked (or so I thought) at 15:01. Going sub fifteen became an invincible wall to me, a physical barrier and I was almost convinced I had reached my limits. I said almost!

Had I succumbed to the perceptions of others and listened to those 'words of wisdom', sub 15 for an Ironman would have been beyond my reach before I took my first step in any race. But hey! I am an Ox. I am perennially stubborn and I knew there were others in my age group, Japanese, Americans, German and Australians who beat me by miles each time. So why could I not match them? Or at the very least get within striking distance? These dozen or so guys, my fellow age group athletes must have been doing something very different to beat me so easily. They must be training right and eating smart. Could that be it? Could it really be that simple?

I re-looked at the way I trained. I read books and triathlon articles. I explored. One of the books I read, the Triathlete's Training Bible by Joe Friel, mentions that in order to swim, bike and run far and fast one must do them right. This is the magic mantra that woke me from my slumber. From that point on triathlon training took a new turn. I went back to basics and started back at the beginning at 72 years old.

To learn new and proper techniques in all three disciplines I first had to unlearn and erase all my wrong techniques and bad habits. Swimming to me is the most challenging as we are by nature land creatures. Water is not a natural playground and I am no exception. Without a coach to check and guide me, my progress was painfully slow and very frustrating. It was, however, very satisfying when I got something right. I was like a child taking my first step except that I was a child in a 70 year-old body. All my training sessions were devoted to technique. It was technique, technique and more technique. When I got into the phase for my Ironman training proper, at least one third of all my workouts were devoted entirely to technique. I also listened to my body and responded to its needs.

Saturday February 28, 2009 was payback time. It was the 10th anniversary of Ironman Langkawi, Malaysia and this was the race in which I intended to put all my relearning to the test. My freestyle swim was still not up to the mark so I had to fall back on my reliable breaststroke. I had recently purchased a custom-made carbon fibre bike that was more aerodynamic than any bike I had ever owned before but I decided against using it for the race. I wanted to find out if I could go quicker on a level playing field and that meant using 'old faithful'.

Come race morning as I stood on the jetty before diving into the water at Eagle Bay, I asked my body to show me what it could do for me after three years of struggle. I then dived into the water and my day of redemption started at 7:45am.

I had a slow but comfortable swim and reached the shore in 1hr 38min. My transition from swim to bike was less than four minutes. Gone were the days of sitting on a stool, washing my feet and putting on elbow pads.

The bike course in Langkawi is tough. It seemed to change every year but was never any easier and always a challenge. There are a number of rolling hills and one long one that we had to climb three times. I was familiar with the other athletes in my age group (70-74) and my main target was a Japanese gentleman by the name of Noritoshi Hamajima. Noritoshi had beaten me by 1 hour and 20 minutes back in 2004.

I knew he was capable of running a five-hour Ironman marathon. I also knew there was no way I could make up such a large gap. But I also knew in an Ironman nothing is certain. There are no guarantees and so I secretly harboured a little hope of being able to beat him on this day.

Noritoshi was ahead of me for the majority of the day until almost 20km from the bike finish I spied a lone rider up ahead. He was not pulling away so I decided to push a little over the next hill. As I got nearer my heart stuck in my throat from both effort and shock at seeing my nemesis Bib #644.

We were in the ninth hour of racing when I overtook him for the first time. He recognized me immediately and took off on the descent retaking his position ahead of me. I always feel a bit nervous speeding downhill and had my hands on the brakes most of the time. But hey ho, on the ascent at the next hill I caught up with him again and noted that he appeared to be struggling.

The tug of war between us continued for the next two climbs and he was finally gone out of sight with about 6km to the bike finish. Disheartened, I consoled my weary body telling myself he would pay for it on the marathon.

I completed the bike ride in 7 hours and 6 minutes – this was a new personal best. As I entered the changing tent to get ready for my run I saw Noritoshi, having just completed his bike ride minutes earlier. Perhaps my assumption might be correct; he was going to pay for it on the run. He might not be able to run a five-hour marathon and this would be my first chance in eight years to win a slot for Hawaii. I was not too worried about another Japanese fellow in our age group. He was too far behind on the bike to pose any real threat. In my mind this was now my race to lose.

The marathon course was made up of five loops of 8km with a 1km out and 1km back to the finish line. My first 5km, a shuffle pace of 9.58kph was the slowest segment of the run. The running legs just would not fire up. They must have fallen asleep during the long bike.

On getting off the bike I was very hungry having had no solid food all day. I took on two slices of orange and half a banana at alternate aid stations besides taking in a small cup of sports drink and water. I also consumed a Powergel for each loop of the run.

Over the next 4km as I headed back to complete my first loop I was clocking 7.42kph. This was more like it, my second fastest pace on the marathon. The first time I saw my Japanese rival was at 6km, 1km after my first turn around. He was on the opposite side of the road on his way to the run turn. Now the mental games began. Was I 2km ahead or was he 6km ahead? This was quite unlikely but worrying all the same. He would have to be running a sub 4-hour marathon to be that far ahead of me at such an early stage.

With hope and anticipation mixed in with a little worry I looked out for him after the second run turn. Again we crossed paths and this time the gap had lengthened to more than 26 minutes. I was running 8.11kph pace and for the first time in the entire race a slot to Hawaii was no longer a dream it was a possibility. The thought of it lifted my whole being. My mind was in a wonderland. I would go to Hawaii and I would bring my whole family.

My long-suffering wife had accompanied me to Hawaii on five prior occasions. My daughter, my son and his girlfriend, all of us would be part of the Ironman Parade of Nations marching proudly with the Malaysian flag representing our country. I was in heaven, living my daydream and then suddenly I was jolted to my senses. I had missed sighting Noritoshi on the third loop while I was away in fantasyland. I reprimanded myself for getting carried away. There was still a long way to go and anything could happen and go wrong. "Don't fuck up," I shouted to myself.

Despite keeping an extra vigil for his approach in the dark, I again failed to spot Noritoshi on the fourth run loop turn. I kept my pace consistent and maintained 8.11 to 8.51kph for about 28km. After the final turnaround and with 5km to the finish line I upped my pace and skipped the aid stations. I ran the last 5km to the finish at a pace of 7.38, my fastest sector ever of any Ironman marathon to date.

With about 300 meters to the finish arch I saw my wife walking on the opposite side of the road towards the same place. She had expected me to home in my usual '15 hour mark'. I shouted out to her and got her running after me. I took the final turn onto the home stretch and wow! The thundering music, the loud cheers and claps from the spectators lining the finish I felt like a hero returning home.

"Faster Aunty, faster!" the crowd shouted to my wife who was trying to keep up with me as she ran the 100 meters of her life that night to join me across the line. As I was within sight of the finish the explosive boom of the emcee came over the sound system. "Sze Mun Yee, 72 years young is 20 minutes faster than his time last year. Malaysia Boleh!"

I had beaten the 15-hour barrier. I had finally scaled my physical wall. What a race I had, it was the race of my life in 14 hours, forty-six minutes and 48 seconds. And the Hawaii slot was the icing on my cake. But as I walked towards the recovery area, my nemesis Noritoshi Hamajima was standing with an official towel on his shoulders and greeted me in Japanese. I did not understand what he said but the sight of the towel was a bucket of ice-cold water over my head. What? He finished before me? The towel was only given to those who finished. They were finishers' towels. My spirit was in tatters, my bubble of pride and victory burst. "Oh well, I least I broke the 15 hour barrier." I told my wife.

I had a bowl of porridge and two beers before bed that night but I didn't sleep a wink. By 6am the next morning my stomach was crying out for real food. Down in the restaurant a fellow Ironman from the Philippines tapped me on the shoulder. "Congratulations Uncle, you are number one in your category. You have won a slot to Hawaii." I later learnt that Noritoshi had dropped out on the second loop of the run. While I felt for his loss I knew he would be back and for now I would bask in my win. What a beautiful start to the day.

I have completed to date in 9 Ironman in Langkawi since 2000, and 15 Ironman races overall including Ironman Hawaii five times and one Ironman China. To succeed and qualify at age 72 (my other Hawaii entries except in the year 2000 were via application) and breaking my invincible wall in the process, wow! What more can I ask for?

Hawaii, here I come again. Who says age is a limiter?

Taking on Marathon des Sables

Marathon des Sables posed a very a new challenge, a venture into the unknown. A 6-day foot race over the Sahara desert in south Morocco covering a distance of 248km, each runner has to carry a backpack weighing up to and no more than 10kg. This pack must contain all their food supplies, living and survival gear for the entire race with the exception of drinking water that would be collected at each Checkpoint station en route. I knew triathlon, I knew Ironman and how to train for such an endurance event, but running in the desert was breaking new ground.

This time around I was running for a cause other than my own, the P3KU Special Kids. Most of the time my endurance journeys are guided purely by an appetite and desire to push my own barrier. Running for the kids provided an extra kick of motivation. Not that I needed it, but it felt good to change things up and channel my energies into something new.

I had no idea what I was getting into. Green to the task at hand was an understatement and the desert banged me up pretty well. It humbled the Ironman in me. I was brought down to my knees time and time again. But I did not give in.

Crossing the desert each day I was in a fog of pain that surrounded my entire being. My body was so depleted that the simple function of moving forward became a herculean task in the arid, sandy, rock-strewn

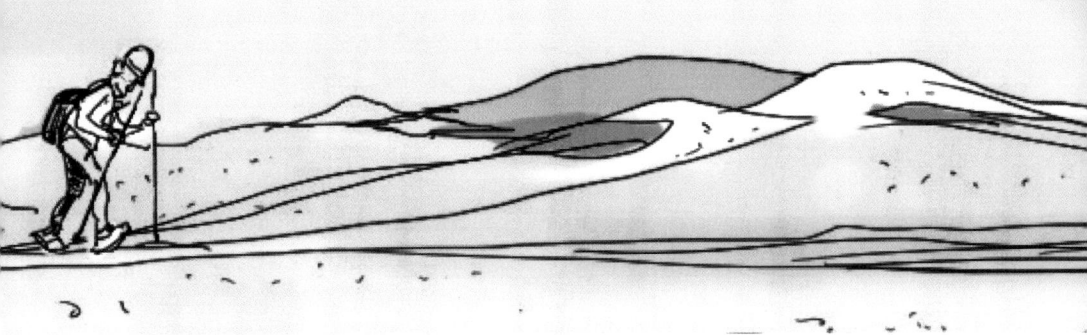

landscape. I experienced some of the most painful moments out there. Progress was slow, so very slow, but I never stopped moving forward.

Many people my age (75) and younger, if faced with similar set of conditions, would give up. There is no shame in calling it quits in Marathon des Sables but 'quitting' (as I keep reminding you) is not in this old man's vocabulary. For sure, I would think about it. The thought was omnipresent in my mind, but it would never happen. For that to actually happen I would have to be dragged out of the desert. And that is precisely what happened.

A race marshal was compelled to pull me off the course and out of 'my' race, thus putting further emotional pain in my already beaten body by ending my physical misery. Yes, I was disappointed for not getting to that finish line but I am more than pleased with myself. I can look into the mirror and proudly say that I gave my best. I did not give up. And most important of all, I learnt what went wrong. I took away positives from the experience and understand that it is no more impossible that swimming 3.8km, riding 180km and running 42km. The underlying fact is I was nowhere near as prepared as I should have been, and perhaps had too little respect for the challenge I took on.

So how did it happen?

I am geared up ready to head to China for Ironman China in May 2011 when the event is cancelled three weeks before race day. Training for an Ironman is no easy feat. You literally put your life on hold for over half a year. Needless to say I like many others who had registered for the event were very disappointed. Feeling extremely fit I wanted to expand my hard earned fitness and was keen on finding a replacement challenge to test myself on.

Around the same time of learning about my race cancellation, I receive a phone call from Lee Chewee Hoe informing me that he, Doc. Tan, his wife and two others have signed up for the 27th edition of Marathon des Sables. The sales pitch is simple: "You have done enough Ironman. Join us for a new challenge."

The bait was laid but I admit it didn't take much for this old man to bite. At the peak of my 75-year-old fitness, three weeks out from an Ironman what did I have to lose and how hard could it really be? I signed up and joined Team 75 Malaysia (named appropriately after my age at the time). Before I could change my mind or 'her indoors' could have a say, a non-refundable booking fee of RM5200 on my behalf was paid by Doc. There was no turning back.

I had hoped to keep this new commitment a secret from my family until I started training at the end of October 2011. But my old lady and son soon suspected something was up from the frequent phone calls and meetings between 'Team 75 Malaysia'. On learning of my challenge – more to their point of thinking – my impending doom, they felt there was only one person who could talk me out of this crazy situation and that was to bring in the big guns, my daughter Joyce.

Joyce is an Associate Professor at Northumbria University in Newcastle upon Tyne, England. We share the same frequency in life and it was she who was tasked with the job of finding out what exactly her old man was up to. Her instructions on finding out the plan (whatever it was) were to talk me out of it. This plan backfired when Joyce embraced Team 75 Malaysia and our quest to go take on Marathon des Sables. Joyce reinstalled some much-needed faith in myself. The negativity in the house at the time had started to plant seeds of doubt in my own mind about what I had got myself into. Joyce's reaction of 'Wow! Dad go for it', gave me the additional strength I needed to get my head around the challenge much to the disappointment of my wife and son.

Once it was evident nothing was going to change, Joyce searched the Internet (I am not at one with the Internet, I am 75 for Christ's sake) and sent me heaps of information related to racing in the Sahara. Standing on the sidelines in the cold, my wife and son finally started to come round to this new crazy idea and turned their objection into support. With my family now 100% behind me my only thoughts to myself was, "I must not fail them."

The journey to the start line of any endurance race is always strewn with speed bumps along the way and the path to Marathon des Sables was no different. Prior to dropping RM5200 on the event I had signed up to take part in Ironman 70.3 Sri Lanka. I saw no reason to cancel the trip and so headed to Sri Lanka in February 2012 for an extra training day. The race was the start of a run of red flags that tried my patience including losing my sleeping bag two weeks out. How you lose a sleeping bag I do not know, it appeared something was trying to stop me from making the trip. I managed to borrow one at the last minute from a previous des Sables participant. His bag was a 15°C comfort zone compared to my -4°C – a huge difference but it would have to do.

It was then the turn of the one of our team members, Dr. Jigit Singh Sidhu to be struck by bad luck. He misplaced his ECG medical certificate upon arrival in Paris. The error cost our team a one-hour time penalty imposed by the race organizer, and a dent of 200 Euro to Sidhu's wallet to undergo a new medical by the race doctor. The third red flag came when Doc's cooking stove came up faulty and mine with all the solid fuel tablets went missing from my backpack. Our entire team was left to rely on Chewee Hoe's tiny stove. It was a less than encouraging start to our race.

Upon arrival at Ouarzazate airport in Morocco we boarded the official bus for a 3.5-hour ride to the Bivona Base in the desert 220km from the airport, 45 minutes of which saw us being bounced around in the back of the truck as we went off road across the landscape of rocks and sand. It was a free for all at the truck pick up. First come first served, only the young, fast and strongest got a seat. While the organizer had done a superb job throughout the entire race, the journey on those army trucks to Bivona Base was a less than civilized affair.

Two days and two nights were spent at Bivona Base going through registration and check-in procedures. My first night spent in the bivouac proved to be quite an experience. There were seven of us in one small tent: three Koreans, a Kiwi and us three disciples of Team 75 Malaysia. Our sleeping space was roughly the width of our sleeping bag with a little elbow room on each side allowing about a meter of space. It was a cold and windy night, the coldest it had been in three years and I had to wear extra clothing plus my wind breaker to try and keep myself in the comfort zone. To add to my discomfort the howling wind blowing sand over my face meant I did not sleep a wink. Lying on that hard and stony ground without a pillow unable to sleep was the last place on earth I wanted to be but I had no choice, I had brought this upon myself. With thoughts of the cold night still chilling my body come morning, I decided to carry extra clothing in my backpack to combat the cold, thus shattering my initial target of keeping my pack at 9kgs. At the start of the race, my pack weighed a little over 10 kg.

Day 1 April 8, 2012
Stage 1: 33.8km

After a short briefing by the race director the race is flagged off at 9am. The start is from no man's land, deep in the desert. There is no fanfare and no spectators – just four hundred odd volunteers supporting the event and various media. Despite the plain setting, moods and energy are lifted from loud speakers pumping out music. With a helicopter circling above ready to catch the start, the magnitude of what I am about to undertake hits me and when the start gun sounds the start of the race I, like many others, dash off like a madman on a rush of pure adrenalin.

My mad rush does not last very long and reality soon kicks in. There is no way on earth I can run with a 10kg pack across rocky terrain and scale sand dunes. Very quickly I come to accept that my best form of attack is going to be a humble brisk walk.

The course features a series of sand dunes, two jebels (hills of sand and rocks) and several black rock ledges. It is the rocky terrain that makes for my greatest challenge. I am not used to being off-road and this terrain is far removed from what I am traditionally used to when racing. I slog over eight hours to finish the stage, missing my seven-hour target by a mile. My reward for the day's efforts is a blister on the ball of each foot that the field doctor bursts to drain out the fluid. Iodine is then injected to prevent any infection. My feet are taped up the following morning before the start of stage two.

Day 2 April 9, 2012
Stage 2: 38.5km

With the mercury almost hitting 50°C, searing heat and strong winds blast my body all day. There is simply no respite from the harsh elements. For 38.5km the weather and the land challenge me. Starting out on a rocky ledge I have to navigate over a series of dunes followed by a long, white salt flat before following a riparian that is holding residual water and mud. The mud clogs up my boots adding further weight to my body and makes progress harder and slower.

I am finally near the day's finish. Just 2km across and up and down sand dunes and I am there. Easier said than done - inhibiting my progress small sandstorms form out of nowhere and keep circulating, reducing my visibility at times to about half a kilometre. It takes nine long hours to complete the stage. The upside is I actually feel physically okay; this is a valuable positive I take away from day two.

Day 3 April 10, 2012
Stage 3: 35km

Racing in heat is something I favour over the cold. Give me heat over cold any day. But the heat in this desert is really something else. There is nowhere to hide. I am exposed to all the elements and wake up to a complete replica of day two. I assume it is hard enough to walk over dunes in 'normal conditions', whatever they may be. Each day I am subjected to being blasted from all sides by sandy wind gusts that leave their tiny grainy deposits of sand over my entire being.

On day three the wind never leaves my path. The sandstorms it creates in its wake cause much of the course to disappear and for someone who is towards the back this means I am left with no footprints to follow. One kilometre after the second checkpoint the visibility is reduced to less than twenty metres. Once again I somehow prevail and make it to the finish. Today was an eight-hour day, another long day at the office but I am still hanging in there.

Day 4 April 11 & 12, 2012
Stage 4: 81.5km

Day four is the longest stage, so long that it carries over two days. This is my D-day for the entire race. If I can pull through in one piece, the race will be mine, or so I thought.

The wind in 2012 is so ferocious that it is later dubbed 'the year of the wind'. It is a phrase that has been used a couple of times before in the race's 30-year history. Marathon des Sables is about sand, sand dunes, sandy riverbeds, dunes and a rocky terrain. 9.1km from the start of day four there is a 1.2km rocky hill with an average gradient of 17%. I find it extremely challenging to get to the top and many times opt to go down on my hands and knees to negotiate my way up. I spend two long hours to cover the distance at times moving on all fours to safely reach the peak. On getting there my torment is replaced with sheer joy at the breathtaking views I am rewarded with.

What goes up must come down. And if I thought going up was tough, coming down the 20% glissade is equally treacherous. I am more than relieved when I finally and safely reach the bottom.

Despite the slow progress on the glissade I make it to Checkpoint 1 (11.8km) and Checkpoint 2 (23.7km) in reasonable time and shape. At Checkpoint 3, the sky is beginning to darken as daylight starts to give way to an oncoming moonless night. Each racer is given a glow stick to hang at the back of our packs, to aid our guidance and identification. The course markers are also set at half a kilometre and marked with a sole hanging glow stick. I set my mind to focus and head to these slim beacons of light.

I feel like I am still making satisfactory progress even after nightfall. At times I am walking with a small group of racers and when I drop back I am still near enough to see and follow the glow sticks swinging from their packs.

The wheels start to show their first sign of a wobble as I approach the halfway point towards Checkpoint 4. My feet, as expected, have already taken quite a beating. I have never really put them through such an ordeal nor asked this much of them in all my years of running and training. The harsh terrain does not offer any respite and as I approach the midway point I can sense my feet getting very tight within my boots. I can also feel searing hot spots underneath the calluses of both heels and more in the balls and four toes of my right foot. It is so bloody painful and getting progressively worse to the point I am forced to significantly slow down from my so-called 'brisk walking'.

So far I have been able to keep sight of the groups in front and use them as an additional way to navigate. On dropping my pace I soon find myself completely alone. Walking up one steep dune I am cautiously negotiating my way down when I suddenly lose my balance and tumble to the bottom. I start to pick myself up and discover the tumble has cost me dearly. I am not injured but I have lost a drinking bottle, my cap and my headlamp. I miraculously find my headlamp after feeling around in the pitch dark, but my cap and water bottle are gone. The tumble has left me feeling slightly disoriented and a little uneasy at my new predicament. I crawl back up to the top of the dune and scour the horizon for any glow from fellow racers in the distance. There is none. And there is none from the course markers. I fear I could be lost.

I sit down and wonder what the best course of action could be. Recalling instructions from the rulebook I attempt to retrace my tracks to see if I can gather my bearings. It is a pointless task, and I knew it from the beginning. The wind is howling and the visibility in the moonless sky is zero. With only my headlamp to guide me I cannot for the life of me find any of my own tracks. For the first time in the race I am starting to feel vulnerable and fear my ability to finish may be in jeopardy. My thoughts turn to the distress flare I have securely cable tied to my pack. On activating the flare, it would mean, Game Over.

Earlier that evening I saw a few flares illuminating the night sky, each flare signals the end of a racer's journey meaning they have succumbed to the challenge. Marathon des Sables sees an average of 10% DNF (did not finish) causalities each year. As I sit pondering these statistics I think of my own flare. It would be extremely difficult to cut loose and this was my intention. I did not want weak moments such as the one I was in to cost me my race. So I decide to stay put and wait, hoping and praying that I will catch sight of someone coming up behind me. I have no clue where I am or even if I am on the correct course but something deep inside makes me stay put and wait. And sure enough I am soon rewarded with the sight of approaching glow sticks and their owners.

I shout out across the sand and rush to join two fellow athletes. At around 10pm that night the three of us safely arrive at Checkpoint 4 (49.4km) beating the cut off by two hours. I have never been so relieved in my life.

We decided to wait until daybreak to resume. To continue in the dark would be tempting fate, getting lost once that night was enough. I might not be so lucky the next time. There is no space in the two Berber tents erected at the checkpoint for racers so I spend the night shivering under the sky. It is by no means as idyllic as it may sound. With no moonlight I am in complete darkness and the high winds end up depositing sand in every orifice known to man. Adding further misery to my discomfort the temperature plummets to 4°C. All the clothes I have and the borrowed sleeping bag do little to keep my tired body warm. Lying still trying to rest, I am then reminded again of the pain in my feet as they start to throb. My right foot is getting worse and I sense trouble ahead.

As day breaks I find Chewee Hoe a few meters away to my right packing up and getting ready to leave. It is yet another reminder of the lack of mercy the desert darkness has on you. We were so close yet totally unaware of the others' presence. Chewee Hoe had checked into Checkpoint 4 just before midnight. He only just made cut off.

It is a little over 10km to the next checkpoint and from the outset my feet are having none of it. The brisk walks that have been my bread and butter from day one are no longer possible and 5km into the day any form of movement forwards is a victory.

On leaving Checkpoint 5 it is another 11km ahead to Checkpoint 6, the 71km point. Any other day and under any other circumstances I can cover 11 kilometres in my sleep. But this is no typical day and I am in severe discomfort with my old feet. By some miracle I reach Checkpoint 6. There now stands just 10.5km between the end of this hellish day and the start of day five.

With my head recalibrated after a brief pit stop I am just about to leave Checkpoint 6 when I hear a rumble of thunder in the distance. Has God not punished me enough? I take shelter and wait the storm out, very aware that my valuable time is ticking away.

The storm is definitely an inconvenience I could have done without. I am fully aware that one second late to the checkpoint and I will not make it to day five and will be going home with a DNF. My mind is focused on the battle at hand but my body, more so my feet are really not behaving. With less than 5km to the finish I gingerly remove my shoes and check the grisly state of my feet.

It is the first time since the race started that I have looked over my feet and the sight is not pleasant. I count nine blisters on my right foot and two on my left. I am very lucky that none of them have burst with the exception of the two blisters the doctor burst on day one. Up to this point Chewee Hoe and I have been walking together but on seeing my feet and realizing I may not make it, I tell Chewee Hoe to go ahead without me. I follow at a snail's pace as gently as I can to avoid bursting any of the raging blisters. That final 5km to the checkpoint goes down in history for me as one of the most painful and longest I have ever covered. I shuffle into the final checkpoint in a time of 32 hours, two hours inside of the dreaded cut-off. The last 81.5km has been a massive physical and mental battle and I feel I am at breaking point. I am the last racer to check in.

Since turning 50 I have competed in over 200 endurance events all over the world. And despite my age, I have never been the last to a finish. Not in my age category nor overall. I was very proud of this fact and as I entered my 60's and 70's I managed to podium in my age group and come in the front 20-25% of the field despite being one of the oldest out there! All good things must come to an end, and I met my Waterloo on day four, Stage 4 in the Sahara Desert. But while my streak was broken my spirit was intact. As I crossed the line I was rewarded with the loudest applause. It was impossible to be sad with my placing. The volunteers, all my fellow participants and the media came out lining both sides of the finish arch to cheer me home.

I was moved to tears for I knew my fellow participants understood the pain and trauma I had been through as they too, hours earlier, had struggled through the same ordeal. I was whisked away by media for an interview and then carried away to the medical tent to have my poor feet attended to and patched up. The doctor in charge told me it would be impossible for me to continue racing the next day. Completely in denial, I told him I would not be giving up having made it this far. The Doc could see there was no sense arguing and gave me two painkillers, one for that evening and one to take the next morning before I set out.

My D-Day
Day 5 April 13, 2012
Stage 5: 42.5km

It's 08:30 in the morning and I am standing at the back of 800 other participants behind the start line for stage five. My body is leaning forward with the weight of my pack but I am managing to stay upright thanks to a pair of trekking poles. I have blisters on my feet like I have never experienced before. Nine on my right foot and two on the left have left me in agony. A painkiller and 'patch-up' from the field doctor last night has done little to alleviate the pain. It is now morning and go time. I pop another painkiller and head out into the desert not willing to let my body stop me moving forward.

Fifty or so professionals speed off and are soon puffs of sand moving in the distance. How they manage to move so fast over such an unforgiving terrain is beyond me. The elite age groupers jog along as best they can, while the majority walk. Leaving the back of the pack, the wounded and the stubborn limp on. This is my group but I was not to be a part of it for long.

A couple of sand dunes later (time was lost to me) as I navigate and limp along I find myself alone. My company is now two Arabs on camelback who follow my tired and weary body from a distance. In the desert the 'SAG' wagon is a camel! These camels are the sweepers employed by the event to keep an eye on the last participant. This is now me.

As the painkiller slowly works its way into my bloodstream I begin to manage a slow walk in-between limping. It is all too little too late. I make my way over the course and come across a small muddy stream. With the doctor's warning resonating in my ears about keeping the bandages dry, I have no choice but wade through and pay dearly the consequences later on.

I make it to Checkpoint 1 in last place and take my compulsory 1.5 litres of water, two salt tablets an energy bar and carry on. It is a matter of just keep moving forward, my stubbornness and strength of mind is my only saving grace at this point that keeps me from stopping.

When I arrive at Checkpoint 2 (22.5km) I am informed that I must start running if I want any chance at all of making the cut-off at Checkpoint 3 (33.7km). My resolve is starting to weaken, what else can I do? Rather than stop and refuel properly I skip my energy intake to save time and carry on, trying, as comical as it seems, to attempt a run.

It is an impossible request of my beaten, fatigued 75-year-old body. I manage at best to muster some brisk walking with limping in-between but as the painkiller starts to subside I become all too aware of how bad my situation is. Checkpoint 3 is just 4.5km away but it could just as well be 100km. It makes no difference. My final warning comes when the Marshal deals the ultimatum: 'Drop out of the race or take another pain killer and run like HELL.'

Well, of course I, of stubborn mind and body, opt for the later. In for a penny, in for a pound as they say and I certainly am not going to be accused of not getting my money's worth. Upon popping the painkiller (my second of the day) I realize 'run like hell' is not going to happen unless I lighten the load of my pack. But it is a realization too late. Twenty minutes later the Marshal stops me again with no choice but to pull me off the course. There is no way I can make the cut-off. I plead in vain to at least let me get there. Instead, he carries me to his four-wheel drive and passes me a can of beer. It was by no means cold but it is the best taste that has passed my lips in more than a week. It also signed and sealed the end of my quest to complete Marathon des Sables. I am just 29km short of the total distance of 248km. The final stage 6 on day 7 was 16km with no cut off time. I feel cheated but also very proud of the adversity I have faced.

It bugs me how I managed to drag myself for an additional 29km over rugged terrain on a hot and windy day when I was supposed to be in the sick bay. It took a crisis such as this to bring out the best in me. I may have been last in Stage 4 of the race and I may have failed to get a finisher medal. But, nevertheless I was amply rewarded. I learnt what my body is capable of if I really push it. A feat thought impossible under normal circumstances.

The icing on the cake was our team of three raised close to RM200,000 far exceeding our initial target of RM100,000 for the P3KU Special Kids.

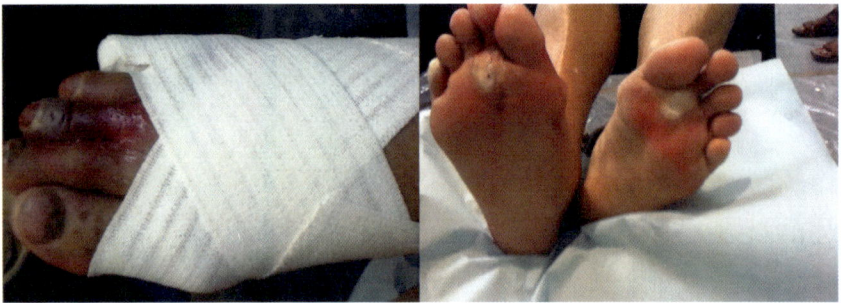

With these feet I dragged myself for 27km until I was pulled off the race.

The long walk.

Team 75

At the finishing line on Day 4.

The M Dot – my priceless beauty

The last time I competed in the Ironman World Championships in Hawaii was October 2000. Since then I have been chasing the qualifying slot in vain. Gone are the days where I could gain entry by mere application, the sport is booming and every year presents deeper and stronger competition vying for slots. Hawaii has become every triathlete's dream and Holy Grail.

In my small age group, only the best get to qualify. The closest I came prior to 2009 was as a runner-up in Ironman Malaysia 2006. I finally secured my place coming first in my category at Ironman Malaysia in 2009. I realized that at 72, the chances of qualifying again would be slim so I wanted to make the most of this opportunity and I talked my whole family into joining me for the first time in Kona for the October race.

My wife and I and my son and his fiancée travelled separately three days apart. My daughter followed us over all the way from Newcastle upon Tyne, England.

The mission was twofold: to get a finisher's medal as a surprise gift for my son whose wedding was the day after the race on the island, and to fulfil the expectation of my family. Easier said than done. It is rare that any Ironman training goes fully to plan without incident. I experienced severe lower back pain in mid July that interrupted a large block of training and grounded me for five weeks. During those five weeks, I could not swim, bike or run. My doctor advised me to give it up.

"The pain will stop you if you stop," he said. His words shot through me like a bolt of lightning. Is he preparing me for life without Ironman? Having emotionally and physically committed so much already to this race, there was no way on earth I would be backing out. I am a stubborn Ox – it just doesn't happen. We finally agreed on a short gap measure for a course of cortisone injections, which enabled me to do a few weeks of light training leading into the race. I made it to the start line, undertrained; unprepared and full of doubt and fear but determined to test the unknown.

There was little rest in race week as I was dashing around with my family, playing tourist. This resulted in soreness in both my hips. I was worried the problem might haunt me during the marathon, but also I knew I had to get to the marathon to find that out! I told my family I needed rest and had a day of rest while they enjoyed a tour of the Big Island. The pain seemed to ease somewhat but it was too little too late. D-day was a different story entirely.

My time for the 3.8km swim at 1:51:37 was over 10 minutes slower than expected. I was one of the last athletes to enter the water after the starting cannon fired. The older age groups were advised to start from the back to stay out of trouble approximately 40 metres back from the start line. I decided to swim wide to stay clear of the 1800 pairs of thrashing limbs. Despite my best efforts I could not avoid getting kicked when rounding the buoys but other than that the swim was uneventful (a good thing) with the exception of some bruising around my right ankle, caused by the rubbing of the timing chip.

The swim is a warm up. The bike will tire you. The marathon is what counts – an experience shared by all seasoned Ironman triathletes.

My past experience with the Queen K has not been great. And my previous bike time of 8:19:32 speaks volumes. Coming into the race my maximum mileage bike session was just six hours. To say that the Queen K and her relentless winds terrified me is an understatement. I expected a slow bike split and I expected to suffer, a lot. But little did I expect the suffering to start the instant I mounted my bike. The pain in both my hips hit me the moment I started pedalling. The sun may have been shining, but on my horizon all I saw was dark clouds and felt a rumble of thunder before 'my' impending storm hit. It was going to be a long day on the Queen K.

I slowed down to see if I could work the pain off. Riders passed me one after the other and just ten kilometres into the bike leg after the initial Palani climb, trouble struck again. My left inner thigh almost cramped up. I had never ever experienced this sort of muscle breakdown before. Why now? For the first time in my sixteen Ironman starts I had a fear of not being able to complete the bike leg let alone meet the cut-off time and run a marathon. Dropping out was becoming a real possibility and starting to cloud my thoughts. As I fought the dropout demon, an inner voice reminded me – "You are an Ironman, an Ironman does not quit," the race is over if I throw in the towel; my dream and that of my family would be in tatters, shattered. I hung onto that thought by my fingertips and managed to keep the dim embers of my dream alive.

I picked myself up and continued to pedal, slowly and painfully. Over the next 40km I was so slow that I hardly worked up a sweat. By kilometre fifty-five the pain seemed to subside and allowed me to up my pace a little. I caught a few riders who had passed me earlier and this really helped boost my confidence. I felt better and began to visualize my goal only to be jolted back to reality by a sudden blast from Mumuku, the legendary wind in Hawaii. That gust of wind signalled the start of a 16km treacherous climb up to the turnaround at Hawi, 90km out from the start line. Fear grabbed hold of me. I was entering Mumuku's torturous wind tunnel and switched instinctively to survival mode. Going up you have a strong head wind blowing in your face, slowing you down to a crawl. Coming down, the same wind is at your back, which should be a blessing except that Mumuku spices it up with unpredictable and fearsome gusts so strong they can easily blow a rider off his bike. She had claimed many victims over the years and I was among those. My arse was so sore mid way up the climb I thought it was on fire. My legs had abandoned me too. The sun was so hot it branded my race number into my arms. I was tired, hungry and thirsty which was partly my fault for missing an aid station.

"Shit. This job is just too tough for me. I am getting too old to chase this stupid dream. Why don't I just quit? Damn that finisher medal!" My mind was so crowded with negative thoughts; it left little room for any sensible reasoning. I was confused and lost. Then I remembered reading a page in a book I had purchased the day before written by Mark Allen and Brant Secunda entitled 'Fit Soul. Fit Body.' It says when the mind is in a stage of confusion, fear and filled with negative thoughts, the remedy is: 'Be quiet. Quiet the mind.' I followed that – silence.' After a while all I heard was the howling winds and the sound of my own breathing.

Finally my inner voice kicked in again. "Hey man! Ironman does not quit. You have gone up there many times before. You can do it again. You want that medal for your son? You better move man. Go. GO!" I finally dragged myself up Hawi.

After the turn it was a 16km descent with the wind at my back. Bigger and more skilful cyclists are able to take full advantage of this 'free speed' and fly down the hill. I had no such luck. Mumuku seemed to extract great pleasure from my misery. She bashed me around so much my bike went zigzagging more than a couple of times knocking the living daylights out of me. Instead of letting my bike 'fly' I had to brake like crazy so much that both my triceps almost seized up. If my climb up Hawi was a torture then my descent was into a hellish nightmare.

It was a great relief when my I finally gained some control back upon reaching flat terrain. The wind suddenly dropped but it was still very hot. As I had experienced years earlier, I was now entering the furnace of Mdm. Pele, the Goddess of Fire.

"You want to be an Ironman? Show me what you are made off?" Give me a break I thought to myself. I made it this far; I won't let you stop me now.

My anger worked wonders. It masked my pain and transformed it into energy. I will show you what I am made of! I hammered the pedals with all my might, my pent up fear and frustration fuelling the attack. My legs shifted into auto mode to a push-pull, push-pull turning the big chain ring. Mdm. Pele finally let me through and I beat the cut off time by just fifteen minutes. It is an understatement to say the bike tired me. It came close to killing me. Meanwhile my family was subjected to some eight hours of nerve wrecking stress and worry of trying to track my movements all afternoon long. Meeting with an accident and not making the bike cut off filled their minds. It was without a doubt their longest day too.

The marathon is what counts. It is where Ironman dreams die. After the never-ending and torturous bike ride and with the pain in my hips and left thigh burning in my mind, I was dreading the marathon. But move forward I must. I wanted the finisher's medal for my son.

Once the sun goes down over ninety percent of the run course is in darkness with a faint white line on the road to guide you. It can be scary to run under such conditions but this was my least daunting part of my day. After what I had already endured on the bike, the run was something I knew and had confidence in and, fortunately, the pain in my hips and left thigh did not come back to haunt me.

My fuel for the entire race consisted of water, sports drink, energy gels, bananas, oranges and more of the same stuff with a few cups of flat coke thrown in for good measure. My stomach had turned into one big fermentation pot fighting its own iron war throughout the day and two cups of miso soup later it was about to explode and I was forced to skip taking anything in for the next two aid stations. With 4km left a fellow runner told me we had just 1 hour and 5 minutes to get to the finish line. The day had been so tough that even my watch had long since quit on me and I had no idea of how far or what time I had left to complete this nightmare.

Realizing that I had enough of a cushion for a little 'detour' I made my way into the lava fields to relieve my erupting stomach in a fury of gas and liquid. Thankfully I had the foresight that day to carry with me two sponges to clean up the messy operation! Relieved and feeling somewhat better I picked up my pace.

Long before I could see the light from the finish area the voice of the emcee and music reached out to me as I made my way home. Lifting my spirits, my pace increased and the noise steadily became louder and more audible. The image of the finisher medal and that of my family waiting for me at the finish arch energized me further into making a dash for the final 1000 metres. One final right turn and I was on Alii drive, the illuminated finish line in sight just 400 metres away. What a sight, what an atmosphere. The narrow street was jammed with spectators on either side, their claps and cheers of encouragement sending adrenalin coursing through my body and tears to my eyes.

For the first time in 226km I was not tired. I felt no pain. I was on cloud nine filled with immense joy, happiness and pride. I floated towards that hallowed arch waving my Malaysian flag and falling into the arms of my wife. I became an Ironman again for the fourteenth time after 16:32:41 of hell.

My son Rodney had a simple Hawaiian wedding the day after the race. The ceremony was held at a place called the Sheraton Cliffs in the Hotel Sheraton garden with a small circle of triathlon friends in attendance. After the ceremony I gave a short talk before presenting my finisher medal to my son. I wanted my family to share a little bit of my experience and let them know what I had to endure to get the medal. Unbeknown to me, my daughter Joyce had made a special finisher T-shirt for me. It had the image of a bull (my birth sign) printed on both the front and the back. Also printed on the shirt was my motto – 'Nothing is impossible', my name, my age and my triathlon CV stating that I am now a fourteen-time Ironman finisher. She was so confident I would get the medal even before I took my first step in the race.

Well, I did not disappoint. I emerged seventeenth out of twenty-six starters in my age group.

To my doctor – thank you for the jabs. I won this round. The M-Dot finisher medal, a beautiful one this year, may be inexpensive to make but it is priceless to me. It is the sum of all my sacrifices, my sweat, my tears, my pain and my blood in getting me to the start line. Many rich and influential people carry fancy titles with their names, some of which were brought but can also be taken away. The M-Dot is mine forever. I hope that my son will someday tell his children and grandchildren how on the eve of his wedding his old man spent the best part of sixteen and a half hours on a journey through hell of the Kona lava fields in Hawaii to get this special wedding gift for him. This medal is now yours my son. Treasure it.

Celebrating the M-Dot with my family.

2001 National Geographic Action Asia Challenge

Since turning 50 I have had the good fortune and health to take part in more than my fair share of endurance events. I have run multiple half marathons and marathons and competed in over one hundred Olympic distance triathlons, 70.3 Ironman and full Ironman distances. In addition, my addiction has also seen me compete in many duathlons (run, bike, run). And I swam the Kapas Island to Marang event four times in total.

The one factor that stands alone in these events is myself, for these sporting endeavours are for the individual. It is just myself against Mother Nature and a clock. Becoming part of a team in an adventure race was something very new to me and an opportunity arose when the National Geographic Action Asia Challenge was staged in 2001 and 2002.

In 2001 the Challenge was held on Pangkor Island. I partnered up with Wong Hock Yim and Chew Chiang Min, both fellow Ironman triathletes and endurance sports junkies like myself. As usual I found myself the senior member of our team. Wong at 52 was twelve years my junior and a self-made entrepreneur living in Ipoh two hours drive from Kuala Lumpur. Chew was in his mid 30's, a young hotshot lawyer who lived in Petaling Jaya, just outside of KL. Our combined age bestowed upon us the honourable title of oldest team. We had zero experience and skill in adventure racing and had not trained together as a team before race day. What we did possess was strong willpower and a high level of fitness. As Ironman triathletes, we entered the race for the fun of it with the notion that nothing could be more challenging than an Ironman so how hard could this really be?

The race began with a mass start. Two members of each team ran and the third member rode a mountain bike along an off-road track. The cyclist was naturally expected to be faster and the plan was he would go ahead and drop the bike at a designated spot and continue on foot. When the teammates arrived one would collect the bike and start riding while the third member would continue on foot until he reached the next bike drop off point and take his turn to ride and then the pattern would start again in a leap frog pattern so each would have a turn to ride.

I was elected to be the first rider in our team. The starting section of the course immediately went off-road over sandy ground covered with knee-high shrubs, thick undergrowth and through a shallow sand pit. My mountain bike skills leave little to be desired and the bike got stuck in the loose sand and I took my first (of a few) tumbles. The rider behind me was a little too close and slammed into my rear wheel upon my fall leaving me with a flat tire. Since I did not carry a spare tube OR a tool kit (the bike was hired) I was forced to run the rest of the way pushing the bike or carrying it over muddy terrain.

The heavy mountain bike soon became a burden instead of an asset and I was left far behind the main bunch of riders. To make matters worse, my teammates ran past the designated drop spot as, noticing the bike was not waiting for them, they assumed I had carried on. Little did they know I was actually behind them.

Upon finally reaching the drop myself and seeing they were not waiting, my misery was further compounded on realizing I was burdened with pushing/carrying the damn bike even further. Luckily for me they soon realized something was amiss and doubled back. Wong took the bike while Chew and I continued to run. This mishap put us at a severe disadvantage. In addition to being the oldest team, the 'easy' cycling leg was working against us and slowing us down. Despite the handicap we surprisingly were not the last team to check into the first transition. The official in charge, however, wanted to disqualify us for two reasons. Firstly, for not carrying spare tubes or repair kits. Secondly, we were now one bike short for the next leg of the race that required all three of the team to ride.

We proposed one member of the team would take turns to run whilst his teammates rode. The official felt there was no way we could keep up with the rest of the competing teams, fearing we may become a liability to the race. We pleaded with him to let us continue and assured him we would indeed drop out if we were the final team to arrive at the next transition. He could not say no to that and we continued on. It was hard work but we made it to the second transition ahead of a few other teams.

"You guys are awesome!" was the surprise greeting from the same official who the day before had been adamant about disqualifying us. By not being in last place we were able to continue on, starting with a 5km trail run.

After the trail run, a coconut tree posed the next challenge. It was required that one team member had to climb up and ring a bell at the top. Being the lightest of the team I shouldered the responsibility. I had much experience climbing coconut trees from my youth and shimmied up the tree belying my 64 years of age!

Never knowing what lay in store around each corner, we next were required to scramble amongst the rocks along the shoreline of the crashing surf. We got through but not unscathed. Navigating our way through the rocks left us with cuts and bruises from barnacles covering the rocks. The final ascent over a particularly large rock landed us back on the beach where we found a row of over twenty inflatable rubber rafts. With no experience at rowing a boat let alone choppy open water paddling, we were all venturing into a challenging new territory. Wong elected to paddle alone while Chew and I partnered up and tried to work together in the other raft.

The simple act of just 'boarding' the raft was a challenge unto itself since the constant pounding of the surf kept throwing us further down the shoreline. After numerous attempts and capsizing twice, we managed to both stay in the boat and start paddling out of the surf. However getting the damn raft to move in the direction we wanted to go was more than frustrating. With no paddling experience and apparently no coordination between us we were soon moving in circles and drifting further away from our destination. The fitness and strong willpower that had got us this far did little to help in a situation which required a skilled technique rather than brawn.

In the midst of our misery Chew began to complain about how painful both his knees had become due to having to kneel inside the raft to execute (what we thought) would to be proper and effective paddling strokes as sitting in the raft our bodies appeared to be too low to generate any power.

The sand on the raft bottom added to the discomfort by working as the perfect abrasive on our knees. I tried shouting to Chew to coax him on and to hang in.

"The shore is near. We are getting there," I bullshitted. But to anyone with half a brain we were in fact drifting further away. And so the whining continued until I could take it no more and blew my top.

"Shut up and keep paddling. Whining is not going to get us to shore. Paddling will." That was our practical lesson on how to paddle a raft. We finally made it to shore where Wong was waiting for us. Needless to say we had lost a lot of time during that sector.

The race ended with a one hundred meter sand ski on the beach to the finish line. Each team was given one pair of long wooden skis that we all had to ski on together. This required putting three feet on each ski. We ended up tying our feet to the skis and executed a kind of lift-walk-lift-walk to the finish in over five hours and, to our surprise were still ahead of many teams.

My first team experience was a pleasing confidence booster. I wouldn't say I was hooked but when the event came round the following year I was willing to sign up again!

2002 National Geographic Action Asia Challenge (Take 2 – The Three Stooges)

In 2002, the race was held in Bukit Merwah Resort near the town of Taiping. Chew could not join us so we roped in Anthony John Lopez, another fellow Ironman triathlete in his late forties. Lopez is a marine engineer and worked for a company in Penang providing ferry services between Penang Island and Butterworth on the mainland. Once again our team, (nicknamed 'The Three Irons", in hindsight The Three Stooges would have been more apt!) was a team of Ironmen and the oldest in the field of one hundred teams.

We lived in three different towns and did not have time nor did we make the time or opportunity to train together. Wong and I blindly ignored anything we had learnt the previous year and vowed to once again go into the unknown with some denial, plenty of iron will and the ability to wing it!

We were not racing for any prize; we raced simply for our own honour so our 'disability' did little to deter us. This year the course was longer and tougher with some new obstacles thrown in for good measure. We had no prior knowledge of what to expect except that kayaking (our Achilles heel) was one of the disciplines.

The race started with a short run to the edge of a small lake in Taiping Lake Gardens. We had to wade through chest-deep water to the opposite side and then trek to the top of Maxwell Hill. As usual, we were the last to start and what waited ahead took us totally by surprise. The water was far from chest deep and as I started my crossing the water was more like neck deep and in some sections totally over my head. I know I stand on the short side but this was ridiculous. Stupidly we followed the muddy trail left by those teams that had waded before us. Unbeknown to us they had churned up the lake's muddy bottom leaving the trail even deeper. Add in continual rainfall from a few days earlier and the water was flowing above normal heights. Weighed down by our trekking shoes, abseiling harness, long socks (to keep leeches at bay) and a backpack loaded with drinks, food provisions etc made keeping my nose above water a tricky task even for a seasoned swimmer.

Despite our own difficulties in the river crossing we caught sight of a two-participant mixed team ahead of us who appeared to be in serious trouble and went to their aid. Although we were proficient swimmers we had no experience in lifesaving and ended up being pulled down by the two struggling athletes who were in a state of panic.

The severity of the situation rapidly escalated becoming almost a matter of life and death. Luckily we managed to pull through and reach shore. After resting a while we managed to continue but sadly the two participants we saved could not carry on and had to drop out. The torment of almost drowning had been too much. We had only just started the day and our first steps into the unknown had already yielded adventure beyond anything we could have imagined. God only knows what lay around the next corner.

We continued on walking all the way to the top of Maxwell Hill. Despite some steep climbs it was the easiest part of the day as we were on paved road. The descent down the other side was a different story. Passing through secondary forest there was no trail just densely thick undergrowth on very soggy ground carpeted with layers of decaying leaves, mud, rocks, fallen tree branches, tree roots, thorny plants, overhanging foliage and insects, lots of insects. It was an assault course from Mother Nature!

Red or white ribbons hanging from tree branches at regular intervals guided our course. For those lagging behind (including ourselves) we had a slightly easier task of following footsteps left by the front-runners. After trekking down one steep and slippery slope to the opposite bank we then had to trek back up the hill and then back down again to the river and then wade back across the other side once more. The process was repeated many times and proved to be a complete energy sapper.

During a descent on a particularly steep and slippery slope we were once again alerted to cries of 'help' from a female participant and immediately went to her aid. She was stranded alone on a tree thinking it would be easier to get down the slope via a tree rather than slide down the slippery muddy slope on her bottom. For the second time that day we turned into Good Samaritans and went to the young lady's aid. Her teammates, nowhere in sight had completely ignored the fact this is a 'team' event and subsequently DNF'd because they did not stay to help.

It was only stage three of a long race and our day had already being quite adventurous. I had lost count of how much time we had spent scrambling over river rocks, but my body was nearing exhaustion. The traversing of riverbeds finally led us back to the top of Maxwell Hill waterfall where we had to abseil to the bottom some eighty meters below.

"Abseiling? Shit we have not done that before!" We knew it was a requirement prior to starting, as our kit included the rope necessary to descend. Knowing and doing however are two completely different things and once faced with the task in hand, it seemed a little, no, a lot less appealing.

"No way man." I said to the official.

The official gave us two options: give up or abseil. There is no quitting, so after a quick 15-minute tutorial we were 'prepared' to abseil.

"It's easy," said the official. Just make sure both your feet land on the rock at the same time. Keep your knees bent, push off a little, and release the rope slightly to descend. To stop, grip the rope. It all sounded easy enough but what he failed to warn us of was the abseil location beneath the waterfall contained very slippery rocks that were not the easiest surface to securely plant your feet on!

Lopez and Wong took their turns to abseil safely down and then it was my turn. My right foot slipped and bang I slammed onto the rock. An X-ray upon my return from the race showed I had suffered three hairline cracks in my ribs. Despite the mishap I made it down to the bottom and from there we jumped eight meters down into a pool where the fall finally ended. I was in obvious pain from slamming into the rock but not continuing was not an option – nor was telling my teammates of my predicament.

From there, the race took us once again onto a trail into more secondary forest up a small hill. We had no idea what lay in wait at the crest of the hill. That was the ironic 'joy' of such a race. You never knew what rounded the next corner. When we finally reached the top we were surprised to see a long line of participants in front of us. There must have been at least ten teams with more queuing up behind. The challenge that waited was called the Flying Fox, a contraption that required a participant to slide to the bottom of the hill suspended from a steel cable. It seemed the 'human traffic jam' was caused by an accident involving a 39-year-old fireman from Hong Kong who eventually (I am saddened to learn) succumbed to his injuries. After more than an hour of waiting a few impatient 'racing' teams confronted the official who then advised those teams who wanted to, to trek down the hill to the next stage as he could not tell us how much longer we would have to wait. So down the hill again we slogged to the next transition and the mountain biking stage.

The first sector was quite treacherous. The downhill track had been carved out by rainwater rushing from the top. The fast flowing water cut deep grooves along the entire stretch; exposing rocks, sharp stones, sand, tree roots and pot holes. With no real mountain biking experience (with the exception of the previous year), and riding on a rented bike that did not fit my small frame I had a nightmare trying to handle the cumbersome beast and while trying to avoid a rock my right pedal somehow got stuck and snagged a tree root flipping me off the bike. For the second time in my life I dislocated my right thumb due to falling from a bicycle. My adventure was fast turning ugly and (in my opinion) life threatening.

The trail continued through some undergrowth with Lopez leading the way. The ribbons tied to branches were still our point of guidance but Lopez had managed to miss a few and we ended up getting lost. Doubling our workload we had to backtrack our steps and start again on more than one occasion thanks to Lopez's mistakes.

The final stretch before exiting the route was flooded and we were forced to push our bikes and wade through knee-deep water. The mountain biking discipline ended with a short session of orientation in an oil palm plantation. A compass kept in Wong's backpack turned out to be a totally worthless tool as the needle had become caked with mud. I had asked Lopez before the race if the compass was waterproof and he assured me it was and prattled on about 'I should have no reason to doubt him and I should know to trust him as he is a marine engineer.'

We managed to borrow a compass from the on-site official and we very unwisely allowed Lopez to once again lead our team. We didn't have the utmost confidence in his abilities but since I could not see without my reading glasses and Wong did not read English we really didn't have any choice. The compass readings were supposed to lead us from one transition to the next where we would then find a token. This token would contain instructions about what we must do next. A compass is not foolproof especially if the person using it is a fool! Once again Lopez led us a merry dance for about twenty minutes failing to find our token which ended up being just two palm trees away. We were lost and Lopez was clueless, I was blind and Wong was confused. And then along came our saviours!

A young female team led by Nadia Lim, whom we had overtaken earlier in the day, appeared at the scene of our confusion. Wong noticed that her team too carried the same blue instruction card that meant they were also looking for the token. He suggested we follow them and sure enough they led us to our token in no time at all despite their protests.

It was with no thanks to Lopez and thanks to Nadia and her team

You are never too old to take on new challenges

that we were saved from a DNF. I discovered much later from Lopez's wife Catherine that without his reading glasses, Lopez is also blind. I also discovered that yes, he is an engineer but one who looks after diesel engines. He was no seafarer. It was my fault as much as his for getting suckered into the word marine and interpreting it into something he was not.

Upon completion of the mountain biking stage, participants ran onto a golf course, which led to a bridge. We then jumped into a lake five meters below and swam to shore where Wong found himself sinking under the weight of his overstuffed pack! Lopez and I helped get him to shore where we then started to lighten his load by eating the fresh supplies he had packed, much better than Power Bars and gels!

After the brief snack stop, one member of each team was required to row a boat blindfolded to a designated spot guided by directions shouted to him from his team mates. Wong took up the challenge and we somehow (I still don't know how) successfully guided him to shore.

The end of the race was near but the concluding disciplines were our Achilles heel; bamboo rafting followed by paddling an inflated raft and kayak to the finish line. To get the bamboo rafts, participants had to wade through waist deep water for 500 metres. It was a difficult 500 metres due to swampy undergrowth and debris that would cut and scratch at your legs. It was a challenge that was not meant to be but due to the continuous heavy rains preceding the race the rafts had got moved. We paddled our bamboo raft back to where we collected our inflatable rafts, two for each team. Wong took one and Lopez and I got in the second.

I finally felt like we were safely on the home stretch. It was early in the evening and the sun was setting. The temperature had fallen slightly and there was a slight breeze in the air. I was looking forward to a well-deserved rest and told Lopez to prepare himself for a few well-earned cold beers. The 'marine' engineer loves his beer and has a large capacity for the stuff.

Shortly after we had started paddling I had the funny feeling our bodies were sinking lower in the raft. The inner sides of my biceps kept rubbing against the inflated tubes on the sides of the raft as I paddled.

You are never too old to take on new challenges

"Hey! Lopez, something is wrong. Do you feel it?" I asked.

"Ya lah. The hull is sagging, we are sinking!" he replied.

To confirm our suspicions a hissing sound was coming from the front end where Lopez's' feet were. Air was rushing out from the valve used for inflating. Lopez had accidentally kicked the valve stop clock. We managed to plug the stop clock back but a lot of air had already been lost and hence greatly impeded our progress. Well, the cold beers would just have to wait. When we finally made it to shore Wong was enjoying a catnap having arrived long before us.

Before embarking on the final challenge, we took and flunked a quick general knowledge test whereby we had to identify three snakes. We failed dismally and the penalty was thirty push-ups each plus carry a pet python overhead. My body was just about ready to give in, I just had one last 'kayaking' hurdle to overcome.

Wong as usual got into his kayak solo and disappeared into the fading light in no time. Lopez and I paddled together. He was the team workhorse and one of his duties was to support me, the 'old man'. We had to paddle the kayak to a landing deck on the opposite side of the lakeshore. Lopez led at the front while I steered at the back.

Before we could even warm our seats the kayak capsized. We managed to roll it upright but getting back in deemed impossible. We swam and pushed it back to shallow water, bailed out some water, got back in and set off again! Despite the set back we were kind of doing okay as I noted there were still teams behind us.

Just when I was starting to visualize an ice-cold beer and the bright lights of the finish line I was jolted from my daydream and back in the water! Capsize number two! Shit, I thought to myself. We were much further out this time and it took twice as long to get back to the shore, empty the water, get back inside and start all over again. Teams that we had long since passed were now beginning to capitalize on our pathetic kayaking skills. Now I know I said we entered the race with the sole aim to take part but the male ego and competitive spirit prevails and we did not want to be last!

You are never too old to take on new challenges

"Fuck. This is no good Lopez!" I let my frustration be known to him but it was not the end as the damn kayak started to rock and roll from side to side again.

"Don't fucking move." I yelled to Lopez. I shouted so loudly that I not only startled my teammate but also those approaching teams around us.

"Just sit still and do not paddle," I commanded. In my mind he was the cause of both capsizes. For some reason that bloody man just could not sit still. He twisted and turned and shifted from side to side which caused the kayak to rock and roll precariously. Perhaps he was suffering from seasickness. Whatever it was that was ailing him, this workhorse was becoming a bloody liability. As the oldest man in the race and despite my injuries, I was forced to shoulder the entire load and solo paddle our kayak to the finishing platform on the opposite shore.

The pain in my rib cage was increasing and restricting me from plunging the oar deep into the water to get a strong stroke. I was merely skimming the surface of the water and our progress was painfully slow, literally and physically. On the bright side we were moving in the right direction and capsizing was no longer a threat as I had Lopez sitting still. He had gone very quiet after my outburst and did not dare move. We finally made it to the platform by nightfall.

The deck was about five meters above the kayak so we had to climb up via a cargo net that hung at the side. It was here I met my Waterloo. I simply could not hoist myself up as the pain in my ribs had become too much to bear. Lopez lifted me from below while Wong who had arrived much earlier pulled me up from the deck. For the first time in the entire race that lasted over 11 hours the workhorse pulled his weight and delivered. For that I forgave him.

We held hands and ran the final 200 metres to the finish line together. Despite all our misadventures, mishaps, de-tours and the handicap of being the oldest team with the least skills and experience in adventure racing we did not come last.

Later that evening we numbed our tired bodies with beer and retraced the day's events. We could not help but laugh at ourselves for the predicaments we had got into. Fuelled by alcohol we could also not avoid arguing, cursing and laying blame for our goofs on everyone but

You are never too old to take on new challenges

ourselves. Wong and my finger pointed to Lopez. Here we have a marine engineer who has no clue to use a compass. Neither can he paddle a boat.

"Hey – Lopez! Which naval college did you go to?" I shouted.

"I only look after marine engines." he replied.

"Why did you not tell us before" I asked. "You didn't ask," was his quick response.

To this day all three of us are still bound by our mutual loves, both for endurance sports and the medicinal amber liquid known as beer.

The three stooges.

The 8th Asian Triathlon Championship, July 11th, 1999 – Korea

It is 8am and the screech of an air horn signals the start of the 8th Asian Triathlon Championships breaking the nervous tension hovering over 470 waiting athletes. As I follow fellow age groupers into the choppy cold sea off Sokcho city in South Korea I quickly find myself back on the shore before I can even execute one stroke. The powerful breaking surf along the shore is sweeping many participants back onto the beach. Its force is so strong my body is tossed in the sand and rolled around like a piece of driftwood. With every athlete in a full wetsuit, to the passer by the spectacle could easily be mistaken for a mass of beached sea lions struggling to get into the ocean.

I have sand in my ears and my mouth and trapped in my less than snug wetsuit. Before I have even started I am chafing due to sand caught in hard to reach places! My second attempt to dive into the ocean is met with similar fate. It is only on my third attempt that I am lucky enough to break through the surf and begin my race.

As I surface for my first breath I find myself further than expected from shore, carried out to sea by swift receding water. The water is cold and choppy with three to four meter swells churned up by high winds. My wetsuit, brought the day before, does not provide a good fit. It is a 'Long John' type, which is sleeveless with gaps between my armpits and chest. I am paying the price for buying and wearing new kit on race day, a lesson many triathletes, including myself, never learn.

The cold however is the least of my problems. Caught between swells, I am routinely being lifted up and tossed around like a rag doll and unnervingly I can not see any other swimmer around despite the fact there is supposed to be 470 other athletes in the ocean going in the same direction as I. My panic level is rising, the conditions are undoubtedly the roughest I have ever swam in and the cries for help coming from various directions are doing nothing for my nerves. It is a chaotic situation that is later magnified by the statistic that 27% did not make it through the swim.

In hindsight, the swim should never have been allowed to take place. Many swimmers became seasick and a few came close to drowning, even the water rescue had trouble staying upright.

I could have followed the herd and given up but it dawned on me that although I may be scared and cold I was not drowning. I knew that much about my situation. I had not swallowed any water and the wetsuit no matter how ill fitting; it was helping keep me afloat. So why should I give up? Let's see what happens next I thought to myself.

While treading water I look around to assess my situation and see that I am indeed alone in a very rough sea. I gradually calm down and take control of my situation and the state of panic subsides. All the participants including my direct competition are in the same boat as I. It is a level playing field. Maybe this is an opportunity for me to profit from if I can find my way out of this. In-between swells I tread water, floating on their crests gives me a clear view of the turnaround orange buoy some 375 metres from shore where we exit and run 100metres on sand before re-entering for a second loop – a prospect I am not looking forward to. The journey to shore is like riding a roller coaster. One moment I am floating at the top of the waves, the next I am back at the bottom of the sea. Forwards I swim and backwards the swells push me. I finally make it to the turnaround buoy and can focus on getting back to shore.

My route to the shore, while less taxing on my engine, is adrenalin charged since now I am moving with the tide rather than fighting against it and the movement is rapid! I am almost there when an incoming swell picks me up and throws me the remaining distance to shore. Not quite the arrival I expected but none-the-less I am now on land and running across the sand to start my second loop when the technical race director notifies me that the swim has (for safety issues) been cut to one loop and I can proceed on with the bike. Phew.

When I get to transition there are still fifteen bikes on the rack for my age group of 60 and above. Wow, I must have been the first out of the water for my age group. What a pleasant surprise after such a hellish swim. My spirits lift. My perseverance has so far paid off.

After such a tumultuous start to the day the 40 kilometre bike course is tame in comparison and goes without incident. Onto the run and the surrounding strong winds that created such mayhem in the swim now provide light relief rather than impede my run efforts and I cross the finish line in 2:48:53 and champion in my age group.

I find out after the race that five athletes in my age group did not make the swim. Mother Nature had indeed lent me a helping hand that day. The remaining nine athletes who survived the swim were so traumatized and bashed up from the conditions that their goals were realigned to just finish rather than challenge for any podium spots.

I said thanks to Mother Nature and my years of learning in overcoming elements that saw me the victor of this race. I have taken lessons from each and every race irrespective of the outcome. If I did not do well (and there have been quite a few) I soon learnt not to dwell for too long, it is important to learn from failure as much as success. If it was weakness related this is something I had control of and I would focus my efforts on strengthening the weakness. If it was Mother Nature related, then alas, it is out of my control and sometimes you win and sometimes you lose. This round I won!

This is the reason I keep on going today even at the ripe old age of 79!

CHAPTER 6

Lessons in life, training and the power of friendly competition

Tomo and me

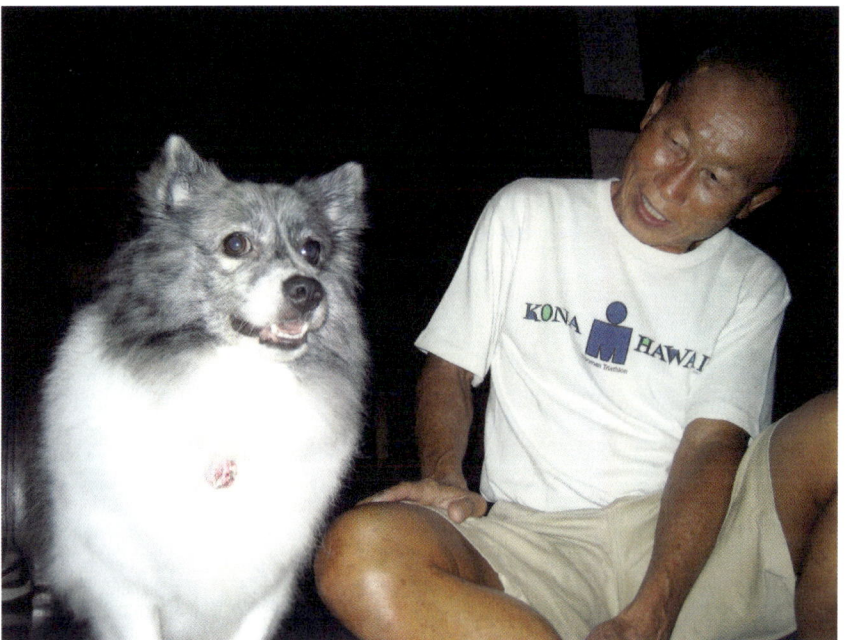

Tomo and me enjoying each other's company.

One Sunday evening sometime in May 2004 I was in our garden tending to the plants when my son Rodney and his wife returned home and called out to me. I looked up from my gardening to see following behind them a little black ball of fluff with a snowy white chest, neck, stomach and paws and a white tip on his tail that looked like it had been dunked in a can of white paint.

His name is Tomo, Rodney informed me, a shortened version of Tomotachi, which is 'friend' in Japanese. The arrival of Tomo was a complete surprise as I had twice turned down their request to keep a dog in the house. To say I was caught off guard by the puppy's arrival was an understatement.

I have no problem with pets, especially dogs. I used to breed boxers back in the 70's. But our present home provided no fenced-in area to allow a dog to run and I was against keeping them in cages or tied up all day. So I was rather annoyed at this sudden introduction. I stopped what I was doing and watched little Tomo who seemed rather excited at this new environment. After a quick sniff about he went about exploring the garden following closely behind Rodney and his wife.

Rodney and Joyce's apartments are located on the ground level within my main house. It is not unusual for many Asian families to live together in an extended house after they are married. Living together but also living their own lives within their own space. A dipping pool cum fishpond towards the back of the house separates the apartments. Direct access to their front doors is via five rounded concrete steps built over the pond. Poor little Tomo slipped at first attempt to cross and promptly took his first swimming lesson. I fished him out, soaking wet and shivering. He appeared so small and skinny in my hands that I could not help but feel sorry for the pup. His timid demeanour and sad eyes quickly turned my reluctance to accept him into sympathy.

"Oh heck, lets keep him," I mumbled. And so Tomo became the newest addition to our family. His path and final destiny in my life was soon to be revealed. Rodney married May in 2002. May was an animal lover, especially of dogs and she very much wanted to have a pet dog. Rodney however is allergic to animal fur and had so far in their marriage held firm against getting a dog. Unbeknown to me, their marriage was in troubled waters and, putting his allergies aside, he promised to seek permission and get a puppy to please May.

My reasons behind not approving a dog were, as explained, because our home was not suitably set up. I also sensed this was a rather uncharacteristic decision on Rodney's part although I knew nothing of their marital troubles.

May moved out of the family home in March 2004 on what I believed to be a trial separation and Rodney had brought her Tomo as part of an attempt to salvage their marriage. Purchased for RM500 from a pet shop in Brickfields, Kuala Lumpur, Tomo and his brother were the last two left in a litter of pups and since Tomo's brother was much bigger and more on the aggressive side, Tomo being smaller and timid, Rodney picked him up and accidently dropped the poor pup on the ground. Feeling bad for their mishandling and sorry for the timid quivering pup, Rodney and May ended up leaving the shop with Tomo.

May had Tomo with her for just a couple of days. She lived alone in an apartment a short drive from our house and very quickly realized looking after a puppy and going to work all day was not the perfect scenario, hence the surprise appearance in my garden a few days later. Since then Tomo has become an important member of our family and to me in particular.

That night I did not have the heart to lock him in the cold steel pet carrier Rodney had brought him to the house in so I put him up in our drying yard, a room the size of a bedroom with an old towel to sleep on. There are two air conditioner compressor units mounted on the floor next to the wall in the drying yard so I blocked both ends to prevent the little guy from getting into the crawl space between the compressors and the wall. I woke early the next morning eager to find out how he had handled himself through the night in his new environment and was shocked and amazed to find him trapped in the narrow crawl space. How an earth did he get in there? It bugged the hell out of me but I was pretty sure he had chosen to worm his way into the little hide out, probably to feel more secure sleeping in a confined space.

When I managed to get him out he made a dash out to the garden and let go the mother of all pees. The poor bugger must have gone through hell the whole night keeping his bladder in check. The comic expression of great relief on his face was enough to warm my heart. I told myself that this little pup is no ordinary dog and I was right. Tomo grew into a neat and well-behaved little dog, although a little cocky at times he has good personal habits and is a joy to all of us in the family. Unfortunately, Rodney, or should I say Tomo, could not save his first master's marriage and Rodney and May finally divorced in 2005.

The arrival of little Tomo as a permanent resident in the house changed all our lives but I felt a special bond with the little fluff ball whom at first I had almost rejected. My first task was to temporarily fence up part of the compound in our house to give him room to move around during the day. Before retiring each night I would let him out to the garden and play with him before confining him to the drying yard for the night. In the morning I would once again let him out to the garden to answer the call of nature followed by more playtime. After his food it was back to the compound for the remainder of the day and thus a new routine ensued.

With love and good food the little bugger grew fast and was a hungry little devil. My old lady and I also took to having to replace our rubber slippers at an alarming rate. Even my pool buoy could not escape the wrath of Tomo and his chewing! I was not angry, how else could we keep the little fellow occupied the whole day when left on his own.

At the age of four months I started training him. Each morning I spent up to 30 minutes training him the basics of sit, stay, come, fetch, beg etc. He was a fast learner and seemed to enjoy the lessons or perhaps it was the treats he was rewarded with for getting his tricks correct. It was then that I noticed he possessed a sharp and sensitive nose. So instead of rewarding him immediately after he preformed a task I hid the treats either under a doormat or buried them amongst the pebbles or sand. He still had no trouble finding them.

Training soon progressed to sniffing out and finding toys, name cards and even currency bills. His scores were pretty impressive and he never failed especially in finding money. As his trainer I was proud to show off his skills to visitors and seeking out money was the main draw. I would normally ask the visitors for a Ringgit note to let Tomo sniff and then tell him to find it. To make sure he got the scent I would wave the note in front of his nose a second time but the cocky little bugger just turned his head away with a look of contempt in his eyes as if to say, "I got it. You don't have to bother me again." Of course he never failed me. And as if to spite me for doubting his ability, on finding the note he would tear it up in front of me. The whole trick ended up costing me many replacement Ringgits to my visitors but it was so worth it to see the look on their faces.

One evening when Tomo was about 5 months old I introduced him to the world beyond the confines of our house. He was a little nervous and unsure to step out of the gate but soon got over it, sniffing and marking his way here and there as I walked him down the road. While sniffing at the gate of a neighbouring home, a large dog came bounding at him with such a loud bark that poor Tomo got such a fright he took off so swiftly and forcefully that his collar slipped and when I turned around he was nowhere in sight. He had disappeared into the dark and would not come to my call. Concerned he would be out all night alone I suddenly heard a loud yell coming from the direction of a dead end. A bungalow under construction at the far end lot had a Bangladeshi worker cum caretaker who slept on site on a sheet of plywood on the dirt floor. He had been jarred awake by a wet tongue licking his face. So shocked at the intrusion to his sleep he jumped up from his bed and let go a thundering yell, scaring the living daylights out of little Tomo and me. Tomo took fright for a second time in as many minutes of the first one but this time luckily he ran back to me for security. The poor little bugger's first venture outside the house was so traumatic that he was hesitant to follow me when I tried to coax him for his walk the next evening.

As for the Bangladeshi, his own experience with Tomo had proved equally traumatic but ended in a happy friendship and Tomo would seek out the Bangladeshi for some extra playtime during his evening constitutional.

Next to the construction site is another large bungalow with two dogs, an old Spitz and a Beagle. Tomo befriended the beagle. So after he had his playtime with the Bangladeshi he would proceed next door and rub noses with the Beagle through the gate as if asking him to come out and play. The little Beagle would respond with a little noise of his own and

would wait for the maid to unlock the gate so he could catch Tomo up. The two would play for a while and then continue to walk with me. This became a daily routine between the two except during bad weather or when I was out of town. Sometimes the Beagle named Dobby would follow Tomo home to our house and stay for a while before going back to his owner's home.

A few months later, Tomo was visiting Dobby's place during his evening walks but Dobby was nowhere to be seen. He made his familiar little noise calling out to Dobby and waited, but still no Dobby. He then walked to his usual waiting place two houses down but still, no Dobby. Tomo went down the slope to Dobby's house and repeated the process but there was no sign of the Beagle.

The next morning, Dobby's owner came to my house to check if I had seen his dog. Apparently Dobby had gone missing on the same day Tomo had been looking for him. It seemed Dobby was lost. He could have been dog-napped or worse still, met with an accident. Dobby the Beagle was never found but for two weeks Tomo continued to stop at his house on his evening walk and would bark for his lost friend willing him to come out and wait for him at the exact same spot every day until I could coax him to continue our walk without Dobby in tow.

Tomo and Dobby came from very different worlds. Both males, Dobby was a pedigree Beagle while Tomo is a crossbreed. Despite the difference in their backgrounds both of them built up a close bond of friendship much to my amazement and envy. Animals kill for food and to protect their siblings while humans sit atop the food chain. Humans kill for greed and power, over jealousy, religion, racial conflict, different ideology and the colour of our skin. If you ever get a chance to watch the movie 'Hachiko', please do. It tells a dog's story that compares their unyielding loyalty, devotion and faith to that of the human. Maybe we can learn a thing or two from man's best friend.

Thunderstorms and firecrackers are year-round disturbances in Malaysia. Like most pets Tomo is terrified of both and our kitchen door bears the brunt of deep scratch marks for not letting him indoors when lighting strikes or the neighbourhood kids are letting off firecrackers during the festive season. Like other dogs, he also hates squirrels and yet lets himself get bullied by them. Our neighbour's cat also gives him a hard time which I am sure drives his blood pressure up time and time again when the cat taunts him safely out of reach sitting on top of a low brick fence. Despite all Tomo's barking and growling the cat totally ignores him. So Tomo tries to jump up and dismally fails so reverts to dashing round and round barking crazily in circles while the cat snootily looks down upon this crazy little dog. His angry barks turn to growls and then wailing out of frustration and still the cat does not budge. Our cocky little prince has met his Garfield.

Despite his shortcomings, Tomo has many virtues and fills our life with joy and laughter. I travel out of town a couple of times a year for

Lessons in life, training and the power of friendly competition | 115

my competitions and when I return Tomo is always happy to see me. Jumping all over me and licking my face and making his little complaints as if asking me where the hell I have been for so long. First order of duty, no matter how tired I am, is to take Tomo out for his walk.

When my family and I travelled to Hawaii for Ironman in 2009, I had to send Tomo to a boarding kennel. Despite his happiness and excitement in seeing us after a long separation he was insecure seeing my bike box still in the doorway at the house, thinking perhaps I was about to leave again. Unpacking my bike after an Ironman is one of the last things on my to-do list as it is for many triathletes, but Tomo sticks to me like a leech until I finally unpack and put my bike away. Only then he will ease up. The poor soul was locked up in a crate for up to 23 hours a day during our absence, is it any wonder he feels so insecure. Any sign of a suitcase or box to him, means that I am going away again.

Competing in the Ironman leaves me with a battered body that aches year-round. I have suffered from severe back lower back pain and on two occasions required long and extended treatment on my back. Despite taking painkillers I still have trouble sleeping at night. My wife is never amused because my twisting and turning in bed disturbs her sleep.

"I can't help it," I would apologize.

"You asked for it," she would grumble back. "Go sleep in the guest room," she demands.

At one time the pain was so severe that I had trouble taking Tomo for his walk and could not cover more than 200-300 meters without having to stop and try and stretch my back. I would call out to Tomo who would be off running ahead to wait and he would look back with concern. At times when I had to bend down to massage my back Tomo expressed his concern by licking my back. This simple little act enhances my love for the little fellow.

The years have been prosperous for Tomo in as much as he has put on some weight (perhaps a little too much for which I blame myself) mostly due to our generosity and love. I also don't get to spend much time with him in the mornings now due to tight workout routines, but I make it a point to groom him once a day, walk him a couple of kilometres each evening which serves as a warm up for my second workout of the day. Before I retire each night I'll spend more quality time with him. Sometimes he will rest his head on my legs while I pet him. Stroking him or just talking to him is a therapy that helps de-stress my aching body and mind. The perfect ending to a day is enjoying a cold beer after a long run or hard workout which Tomo never lets me enjoy alone, no wonder he is getting fat, but I wouldn't have it any other way.

To beat Old Man Yee

At around 10pm on December 18, 2010 a party was in full swing. The climax of the night was the singing of Happy Birthday before the 'birthday boy' proceeded to blow out the inferno of candles and cut his cake.

"Make your birthday wish!" shouted the guests.

An immediate response came back. "My wish is to beat old man Yee and Sofian in next year's Ironman."

The birthday boy in question was Dr. Tan Tah Ming who had just turned 55. A fellow Ironman and an endurance junkie, Doc is also, (in his real job) a successful practitioner. Very much a jovial and likeable chap with a huge capacity for drinking beer, by the time he had disclosed his little nugget of a wish, Doc had himself downed two 500ml bottles of German beer! Dr. Tan is himself an 8-time Ironman finisher, including a one-time Ironman Kona World Championship finisher. He has also completed the Morocco and Gobi desert runs. So in fact, his wish on paper is not unrealistic. In reality however he has never got close to this old man!

Unbeknown to me, Doc has wanted to beat me since the early years of our triathlon careers. How could he let an old man, 18 years his senior beat him? He even has a standing bet with Dato' Ng Joo Ngan to beat Old Man Yee. The bet stands that if he wins, Joo Ngan, who is also his cycling coach and training buddy, would buy him and nine lucky others, dinner. If he loses, then the dinner and the laughs are on Doc.

For many years in a row now Doc has been the one buying the dinners. When Joo Ngan finally broke his silence about his long time standing bet with Doc, it definitely added some spice to my races and an extra rocket up my butt. Come what may, I have always looked forward to my duels with Doc and I have had more than a few interesting ones along the way.

I am a little faster than Doc in the swim. Usually out of the water 5-15 minutes ahead of him in an Ironman swim. Doc would routinely

catch me on the bike, this being his strongest discipline. Training with Joo Ngan had its benefits. Doc would consistently beat me on the bike by 40-70 minutes and that is a big buffer to take into the run. So, going into every marathon I usually had a minimum deficit of 40 minutes to make up. This made my marathons very motivating and (to me) extra exciting. Doc won't mind me saying he is a terrible runner, usually spending seven to eight hours on the run course. The fact that he still manages to finish an Ironman is really amazing.

Our duels usually begin midway on the bike leg where Doc would catch and pass me. Sometimes he caught me before midway, especially if I had a bad swim or in general a bad day at the office. When he had me in his sights and was within shouting distance Doc would whistle a tune so I would know he was within striking range. It never failed to irritate the shit out of me. Perhaps he was trying to lure me into challenging him on the bike and the times when I did try to up my pace in response to the hideous whistling he would happily sit behind me enjoying the free ride. So I had no choice but to slow right down and force him to either reduce speed so much that cut off became an issue or have no choice but to pass me.

Going into the marathon there was always a big cushion of time but I always knew without fail that I would catch him. Such was my confidence of my running ability and his running disability. And so now it would be my turn to become the tortoise. Despite my own struggle at this stage of the race knowing that I was chasing Doc turned my ordeal into hope, fun and anticipation of when I would make the pass.

"Wah Doc, you're so far ahead. Die-lah cannot catch you this time." I would heckle at him when we crossed paths of the looping run. The look of worry was plain to see on his tired and pained face. The smile and whistling had long gone.

"Doc, I am coming," as I caught up with him on lap three of five. He looked back and made a vain and desperate attempt to jog but soon gave up.

"Mun mun lai" (take it easy) he responded in Hokkien dialect.

I patted his back as I passed him. He looked at me with a sad smile.

"Have to buy Joo Ngan dinner again." That was his last and final response before I left him once again before disappearing into the darkness. Despite my own sweet satisfaction in beating him yet again I felt sorry for Doc. He always really tried. He had given his all.

Becoming the subject of Doc's birthday wish was an honour for me. He must really be disappointed for failing to beat me over the past 21

years since we started competing together. His itch is 21 years long. Given his determination and his commitment and with age in his favour, getting Joo Ngan to finally buy him dinner is more than a possibility in the near future. If he gets his weight down and works on his running, I would not be surprised if he hands me my Waterloo in the coming years. If that day indeed arrives I will neither be sad nor ashamed. I will rejoice and enjoy the free meal from Joo Ngan. I will also let it be known that I will keep fighting to maintain my clean sheet until the day I can no longer put my body through this turmoil.

I was excited when Ironman returned to Malaysia in 2014 as it enabled Doc and I to resume our Ironman duel. Sadly in 2015 I had my first DNF in Malaysia. This presented Doc with his best ever opportunity in 25 years to finally beat me but his Achilles heel was once again to be his downfall. By the time I had made it to T2, Doc was more than an hour into his marathon and this was his chance to finally beat me. Tragically this also turned out to be his last opportunity to beat Old Man Yee. All he had to do was get to the finish line before midnight and the glory would have been his.

At the 25km mark, Chewee Hoe broke the news to Doc that "Yee missed the bike cut-off". From a video I saw at his recent wake Doc jumped (as much as you can during an Ironman) for joy, throwing both arms in the air in celebration, when moments earlier he could only manage a shuffle.

"Yes! Old man, I am finally going to kick your ass. Joo Ngan, dinner and drinks are on you this round," I can imagine, was the thought going through his mind. But I could not blame him. He had waited 25 years for this moment to come. He made an attempt to run, but was soon back to the same painful walk. When he too realized there was no way he could make the cut-off he stopped by a roadside food stall and enjoyed some supper and beers before proceeding to the finish line way past midnight. He was once again the last to arrive home – this is the typical Doc we fondly remember, a true legend in the Malaysian Ironman circuit.

One week later Doc brushed his DNF aside and went on to take part in a 6-day Ultra marathon covering 240 kilometres in the jungle in Cambodia. Upon his return he was hospitalized for a cancer operation and had almost half of his stomach removed. When I visited him he was his usual joyous self, albeit a little weak. He reminded me we have a date in the Sahara in two years time where he had hoped to celebrate his 10th anniversary Sahara run. I too have unfinished business there and hope to be, if not the oldest, one of the oldest, to complete the run. Doc also warned me he would kick my ass the next time we duel in Langkawi. I had no doubt he would as age was now leaning very much in his favour, and he was very tough between the ears.

At 9pm on Valentine's Day I received an SMS from Lee Chewee Hoe, "We lost Doctor Tan tonight." My shock was magnified further when his wife, Jenny, took the time to reach out to me with the words, "Ming passed away peacefully at 20:26 tonight in my arms and in the arms of Jesus. Her words hit me with a magnitude of 10 on the Richter scale. I just started to cry. I never shed a tear when my old man and mum passed away but losing Doc, well, it is so unfair. Why do good people always die so young?

My golden years

Back in the 80's I attended a three-day training course. I cannot for the life of me recall the subject of the course but it was related to management and motivation. What resonated with me was a case study the trainer told about a retiree, 'John' (not his real name).

After graduating from high school, John got himself a clerical job in a trading company and worked his way up to become the office manager a few years prior to his retirement at 55. John worked from 8:30am to 5:30pm Monday to Friday and a half day on Saturday each week. He was up each morning at 6am, had breakfast at a coffee shop near his office and was home by 6:30pm each night. This was John's routine for 34 years.

As his final day of work drew nearer John had a new spring in his step at what lay ahead in his new life post work. "Ah soon I don't have to get up early in the morning. I can stay up late and watch my favourite dramas and I'll get my EPF (Employee Provident Fund) money and go overseas for a holiday with my wife."

The day finally arrived and on the said day his boss and staff honoured him with a farewell lunch. John was a happy man on his last day of work and looked forward to a well-earned retirement. A couple of months later, John received his EPF and as promised, he and his wife went overseas for a two-week holiday. Upon his return and for the following weeks, John and his wife occupied their time visiting their son and daughter who were both married and living in different parts of the country. John also popped into his old workplace a couple of times to have lunch with his colleagues. He showed them his holiday photos and of course shared his adventures. It seemed John was really enjoying retirement.

Alas all was not as it seemed and John's 'honeymoon' came to an abrupt end. His working body clock of 34-years woke him up each morning at 6am without fail and without a hobby to occupy the day after a few short months John found his new life just as boring as the programs on the three local TV stations that he had once yearned to have time to watch.

Passing the day soon became an ordeal until a friend advised him to go for morning walks to keep fit and meet new friends. He did just that and wow, what a surprise, on his first outing he met so many other senior citizens in the park. Some walked and some were doing Tai Chi. John got to know a group of them after a few days, he would be in the park by 7am each day five to six days a week without fail. After the walk John and his new-found friends would proceed to a nearby coffee shop to have breakfast and read the daily newspapers and chitchat, exchanging stories about their lives. He would be home by 11am, have his shower and get ready for lunch. For the next few months, this became John's new routine and he started to feel that perhaps retirement was not so bad after all. Despite hearing the same stories and having the same conversations every day, it helped pass the time.

One morning, Ah Chong a retired bank officer in his 60's did not show up for his usual walk. He had suffered a massive stroke. John and his new friends visited Ah Chong in the hospital and were shocked to learn that although Ah Chong had survived, he was now incapacitated and unable to move or speak. For many days Ah Chong's fate was the subject of the daily breakfast table talk among the group. Not exactly a morale-boosting topic!

Not long after Ah Chong's misfortune, Mutu, a retired estate supervisor also in his 60's, failed to show up for the morning walk. Mutu had suffered a sudden heart attack and passed away. The diminishing group of friends attended Mutu's cremation and for the following weeks the subject was tuned into Mutu's untimely death.

"When will it be my turn?" Was the very thought on everyone's mind except perhaps that of John who at 55 was the youngest of the group. "I am only 55, I should be okay," he assured himself. Tragedy soon struck again and this time it was the unexpected death of Ali, a healthy looking guy in his mid 50's. Ali had just retired from government service and he too suffered a massive heart attack. Ali's sudden passing struck a chord with John; they were almost the same age. It seemed being younger was no longer any guarantee against sudden death. John's perception of retirement had turned full circle in a very short spell of time with each new dawn taking him one day closer to that hole in the ground.

When I first heard this story I began to worry too. In the 1980's my business was not fully established and I was not in the best of health, having to visit my doctor every other month. I had no time to pursue any hobby or exercise and so I worried I might end up riding into the sunset like John way before my time was due.

My wake-up call at age 48 changed my life. The process of getting back into shape opened up a whole new world and turned me into an endurance junkie. My new life officially began at 50, the dawn of my golden years. Despite the ups and downs along the way, I have never been fitter or happier. I have never done morning walks, though good for general health, they would never equip me to run a marathon and face the extreme challenges of an Ironman. Years ago I did my run workouts in the early evening among some elite roadrunners at the foot of Gasing Hill. These guys were very fast for my level and would be out of sight before I had worked up my first drop of sweat. Like a thorn among the roses, an old tortoise like me looked odd but it never bothered me then or now. I would draw inspiration from the fitter faster younger athletes. They made me feel as young as they were. I trained hard and still did not catch them, but every narrowing of the gap was a small achievement bringing with it the reward of extra motivation. Unfortunately, time and circumstances did not permit me to continue do my swim, bike and run workouts the same way.

After my retirement at 65 I had more time to work out and so increased my sessions to twice a day, six days a week. I swim and bike three times a week and run up to four times with two sessions of resistance training thrown in for good measure. My weekly volume ranges from eight plus hours during the week of active recovery to eighteen hours, seven to eight weeks out from race day. In my 60's I used to maintain a twenty-four hour workout week but even if 70 is the new 60, my aging body does not take lightly to a twenty plus hour training week. I have very little time for TV and that is the way I like it. The TV is the old lady's department. My exercise is more like a fulltime job to me and I have never been happier. I live each day to the fullest and meet each new dawn with purpose and hope. In fact, every one of my workouts is purposeful. This helps eliminate boredom.

I am fitter today than when I was in my mid 30's. I check and record my resting heart rate and blood pressure each morning before I get out of bed. My resting heart beats at age 70 plus are in the low 50's and occasionally at 48-49. Keeping fit is no longer my number one priority; on the cusp of entering my eightieth year, getting my body to swim, bike and run faster and further with less energy is my newest goal. I eat any food I want and consume any drink I like, albeit in moderation. I hardly fall sick and manage at my age to race half a dozen times per year and enjoy every single one of them irrespective of the results. What more can I expect for a 79 year old man?

People often ask me if I have sponsors to fund my expensive hobby. No, I do not have sponsors and neither have I ever sought for them. I am doing what I love. The satisfaction of doing well is my reward. I don't wish to subject myself to pressure with a sponsor. Besides, I do not think I am worthy of that. Another question often asked is what special food and supplements do I take? I do not take any, although I should sometimes control my diet a little better. But then again, at my age, why should I? I train hard partly for the liberty and pleasure of eating and drinking as I please and, for peace of mind, I take my dietary supplement of multi vitamins. The exception is BCAA (branch chain amino acid), which I take after a hard and long work out to help speed up the process of repairing my body. This is taken together with antioxidants to boost my immune system. If the workout results in sore and inflamed muscles I take one anti-inflammatory capsule to ease the pain and bring any inflammation down.

Another question often asked is – "Do you have knee problems?" I do not. And if I ever do have any pain I seek treatment immediately. Many people cite bad knees as a reason for not exercising. My answer to those people is, learn to swim!

As each year passes by you don't have to remind me that I am getting older but I am still often asked how much longer I can continue training and participating in Ironman competitions. The answer is simple. For as long as I am able and for as long as the passion is still burning to participate there is no reason to stop. Besides, I want to still find my limit. I don't think I have reached there yet. I believe wholeheartedly that

I have potential to keep on bettering myself and these are the driving forces that keep me going.

All living beings exist on earth only in transition. We humans spend the first stage of our lives growing up and learning the skills needed to survive. Life at this stage is relatively simple and carefree. This is the best part of one's life to many. The next phase, lasting thirty to forty years, is a dog eat dog world of continuous struggle to carve out a living. For the lucky ones who make it, they get to enjoy a fruitful and luxurious life. But for the majority, it is a continuous struggle. Despite the huge gap between the super rich and the hard-core poor, this is the period when most of us start our families and bring in the next generation. We chase and accumulate material wealth often at the expense of our health. The final phase of our lives is when we retire. Many are compelled to give back part of what we accumulated to fix our health and to prolong our life span. The rich and the poor are equal in this respect except the rich who can afford to pay for a better health care.

I am no different. But thanks to my wake up call at 48 I am able to live and enjoy a different life than my peers because of Ironman. To me, my real life began at 50. This is my golden era and I will do what I can do to extend this golden period of my life.

I never stop seeking new and more effective ways to train my body to go faster and further economically. My training regime also has an effect in slowing down my body's aging process. Every dawn is a bonus to me. I do not see it as one day closer to that hole in the ground; rather I see a purposeful day, filled with hope and anticipation.

The final ride to my sunset can just bloody well wait!

The long journey

The road to Ironman is long and treacherous. Mine is literally littered with my sweat, tears, pain and blood. Getting to the start line requires six to eight months of long and arduous training of the three disciplines: swim, bike and run. To keep this old body functioning strong I also add in some resistance training for good measure. This is my life, twice a day, six days a week. Along the way I have scaled mountain peaks and tumbled down into the unforgiving depths of its valleys. Up and down, up and down, countless times. At its peak, I am buoyed with confidence and encouraged to train harder to scale the next peak. When I fall into the valley, I question how I got there and must find a way out. I do not get discouraged; I look at these lows as challenges. The whole process is extremely motivating, there is never a dull moment and there are many experiences that have had a great impact in shaping my life after starting this life at age 50.

Did Not Finish aka DNF
DNF is an acronym all endurance athletes dread seeing next to their name. I personally have ten DNF's by my name which is 6% of over 170 races I have taken part in from 1987 to 2015 so not a bad record! My most 'memorable' DNF was back in 1996 at the Ironman World Championships in Kona, Hawaii. It was my second attempt at this race and despite a good swim within the first few minutes on the bike I saw black and almost fainted upon reaching the top of the Pay 'N Save hill. I was forced to get off my bike to recover. Thankfully the fainting spell did not come back during the race but I missed the bike cut-off arriving back to transition seven minutes too late and subsequently was not allowed to continue with the marathon. A year earlier in my very first attempt I completed the race in a time of 16 hours 37 minutes and 21 seconds. Many triathlete friends suspected that my first outing was due to beginner's luck and doubted I would be able to back it up the following year. On top of the list of Doubting Thomases was Mohammed Sofian who on the eve of race day questioned my ability to go the distance and my subsequent failure that year reinforced his suspicions.

That was the only excuse I needed to go back for a third attempt in 1997. This time I silenced my negative friends with a time of 15:24:13. The icing on my cake was I had beaten Sofian in all my Ironman races in Malaysia. We had been competing against each other for ten years from 2000 to 2010 and Sofian who is 21 years my junior is highly regarded as a pioneer and elite in the Malaysian triathlon community. A tough competitor he would never give up in any race, I witnessed him almost crawl to the finish line in two races. I salute that determination.

Another DNF that had a significant impact on me was the year of the great jellyfish attack in the Penang triathlon. This is the only time I quit a race and followed the herd out of fear. The lesson I learnt from this experience was put to good use in the 8th Asian Triathlon Championships in South Korea in 1999. It also made me a better investor in stocks and shares; let me explain...

When the stock market crashed in 1978 it triggered a stampede of people rushing to cash out. Amid the doom and gloom, the smart and the brave and those financially able had a field day picking up quality counters for a song. These were the victors who stay away from herds in a crisis. These are the people who turn obstacles into opportunities. I started dabbling in the stock market in my late 30's trying to grow my small nest egg. Being a naïve follower of the herd and with little capital I could never afford to lock up any money for extended periods so I brought penny stocks and followed everyone else and consequently ended up annually losing more than I made. My old lady repeatedly told me to put my 'egg' into a fixed deposit and forget about the stock market. But I am a stubborn Ox and have never listened to the other voice in our house; instead I listened to the bumblebee in me that kept telling me I would make it all back some day.

I looked at my losses as my 'tuition fees'. Racing the Ironman has also taught me to never give up, to also seek out the reasons of my failures and to work on my weaknesses. Not to fear challenges and danger. They are my opportunities and I have embraced them.

This path set me on a long journey to learn about investments in stocks and shares. I read up on articles in news magazines, investment firms, letters, anything related to the subject. My first task each morning was to read through the financial sections of the newspapers. During this time I became a great admirer of Warren Buffett and his words of financial advice are now etched deep in my head.

"When the crowd rush into a hall, you get out. When they rush out, YOU get in!"

"Be fearful when others are greedy. Be greedy when others are fearful."

His teachings have served me very well, not just in the financial world but also during many of my races, particularly those tough ones. Needless to say his words also helped me profit from my investments and during the Asian financial crisis in 1978/9 I took a very bold step to go against the tide and fished from the bottom. Within weeks after the KLSE hitting it's low of 270 points I recovered all my losses from over the years and made a tidy profits for my family and me.

The mass swim start in an Ironman is one big battlefield where even the strongest and biggest get trashed. I take my time and am one of the last few to get in the water. I begin slowly, swim a little wider for the first few hundred meters to warm up and get a feel of the water before progressing into my normal rhythm. From the back I can see where the stampede is. I pick a safe and clear path through. I apply this principle to most parts of my everyday life. During the long festive seasons, the herd rush out of the city to hometowns and resorts and feast at the restaurants. They pay through the nose for sub standard food and spend countless hours battling queues every step of the way. This is beyond madness and stupidity to me. With a little money, every day can be Christmas and New Year. Oh sure, minus the atmosphere but who cares?

DNF by bike incident
Two DNF's were caused by accidents during the bike leg. On both occasions, I was the victim being hit from behind by faster, larger riders overtaking me. Besides cuts and road rash I had two dislocated fingers.

Lesson learnt – Always expect the unexpected.

DNF by illness
Another DNF was caused by illness – the onset of a shingles attack. Lesson learnt – always listen to your body and be aware of your physical condition. There is always another race.

Accidents and illness cannot be controlled but a bike mechanical is something you can control to a certain extent. My only DNF due to a bike mechanical happened when I thought I was more than adequately equipped to handle a flat. I had two flats mid way through the race. I had one spare tire and two cans of gas filled tire sealant but I wasted the two sealants due to having the wrong valve extensions on my tires.

Lesson learnt – Always check and practice doing the job before a race.

Always check the course route

I completed Ironman China in 14 hours 40 minutes but was classified as a DNF because of a major boo-boo on my part in the marathon by confusing part of the 70.3 course with the Ironman course. I still ended up running the correct distance but was classified as a DNF as I had not followed the correct route.

This was the first time event for the race in Hainan Island, China. To complicate the matter, two events were held together at the same place and date with the Ironman 70.3 (half Ironman distance) flagged off two hours after the Ironman start. The evening crowd in the park and the inefficient traffic control added to the confusion for those doing the full Ironman. But I only had myself to blame for not checking out the course before the race.

Lesson learnt – Do not take things for granted. I may be an old hand at the job, but certainty is never guaranteed.

Fainting spells

Following my first fainting encounter after biking up the Pay 'n Save hill in Kona, Hawaii during the 1996 race, I started to experience regular bouts of dizziness followed by vomiting, sweating and diarrhoea. The attacks were short, lasting no more than 30 minutes but it scared me, as I knew I am fit and healthy. I went through thorough examinations by a neurologist, a cardiologist and an ENT specialist besides my regular GP. None of them were able to tell me what was causing these fainting spells. Their common advice was stop swimming and cycling. At my age I should go for morning walks instead they advised. So after paying hefty consultation fees I was left to go riding off into my sunset. Morning walks, my arse! But I did start taking it easier due to the cloud of uncertainty the specialists had built up.

One afternoon after lunch with two friends I was about to drive my car out of the car park when I suffered another attack. I opened my door and vomited into the drain beside my car. I saw a clinic nearby and I went in to seek treatment immediately. The doctor on call examined me and found nothing wrong. However, he told me that he had come across a similar case with a marathon runner. Like me, the doctor found the patient normal. But the similarity of the case to both of us as endurance athletes was something worth exploring. My problem could very well be sports related not age related. The conversation with that doctor lessened my worry. I eventually learnt the cause of my fainting spells from two articles published in a triathlon magazine written by a doctor who had carried out research on endurance athletes, particularly Ironman triathletes. He said the cause of the fainting spells is due to a temporary deficiency of magnesium in the body, especially among athletes who perspire abnormally heavily. Well, I sweat a ton, no thanks already to the humid and tropical climate I live in. So now before I go on a long bike ride lasting more than four hours and above or a long run over two hours I take one 400mg magnesium tablet and another tablet following my workout. I have not experienced any more attacks since starting this routine.

Lesson learnt – If you are not happy ALWAYS seek a second opinion. And never give up hope.

Accidents
Over the years I have had my fair share of accidents, mostly occurring when on the bike.

The worst bike accident occurred during a training ride one Sunday morning a few years back. As I set out from home at the Tropicana Golf and Country Resort I have to ride through a tunnel. There is a drain about two feet wide running across the road at both ends of the tunnel with a metal grating covering the drain. Almost all gratings on roads in Malaysia are not cyclist friendly. The bars of the grating run parallel to the road with gaps between the bars wider than a bicycle wheel, so in order to safely cross the grating you have to steer the bike at an angle. On that fateful morning, my front wheel caught between two bars in the grating and I flipped over. When I regained consciousness, I found myself lying by the side of the road surrounded by two security guards from Tropicana and a couple of motorists. Besides the cuts and bruises I had sustained I was bleeding from the mouth and my helmet was cracked from the impact of hitting the kerb. I lost four teeth and suffered cuts on my lips; gum and the inside of my mouth that saw me go through four dental implants, a process that lasted six months. The total medical bills amounted to over RM28,000. When I submitted my insurance claim, I was paid a pittance sum of RM2400. The fine print in my insurance policy stated the company would only pay for the first two weeks of medical expenses. All my life I have been paying my dues to the insurance companies without claiming a single cent from any of them. When I was compelled to make a claim that was what I got. It was like a punch to the gut. No wonder the insurance companies are so rich.

Lesson learnt – Always read the fine print. Selling features are always highlighted and presented in bold letters in any advertisements and leaflet whereas T&C (terms and conditions) are, without exception always in very fine print so much so you need a magnifying glass to read them!

My most recent bike accident came during a four-hour training ride for Ironman 70.3 Putrajaya, 2016 I was hit from behind by a small car driven by a Japanese lady. The accident happened midday on January 17th, just a kilometre from where I live. I was flung to the centre of the road and there I lay in shock. Luckily the Toyota SUV coming from behind was able to stop in time. At the time I assumed that my injuries were purely superficial cuts and road rash, and the main initial upset was that my custom GURU bike was damaged beyond repair.

A few days after the incident I found myself unable to walk. Following a six-hour visit to the medical centre it was revealed that I had torn ankle ligaments in my right foot. The doctor advised no running for six weeks and no biking for four weeks. I also could not swim as kicking proved too painful and aggravated my foot. With my race in Putrajaya closing in, not being able to train and with no bike I felt a huge void. For a while I was in self-denial but when the ankle flared up (four times post accident) due to my impatience I had to accept the hand that had been dealt me.

This stubborn Ox has finally been forced to his knees and to come to his senses. So Putrajaya was out, I will take a break. There is no more pressure. Just another round to the doctors tomorrow!

Always read the Fine Print
Another bad experience I had involving Fine Print was with a national carrier for two air tickets I bought. They were return air tickets from KLIA to Langkawi for flights departing on February 20 and returning on February 25 2008. I purchased the tickets in November prior with the cost per ticket being RM404 for a normal fair one way and senior citizens fare on the return. I cancelled the reservation within days of my purchase as I found out we could fly a budget airline at a quarter of the cost, which was also more convenient and practical flying from the old city airport a 20-minute taxi ride from my house.

To cancel my tickets I paid a RM65 cancellation fee and instead of refunding the balance of RM339 for each ticket I received two 'Miscellaneous Charge Order' (MCO). Over a year later I tried to use the MCO only to find out that they had expired one year from the date the original ticket was issued. Further fine print that I had failed to put my glasses on and read.

Is the glass half full or is it half empty?
Either way one looks at it, is correct. Ironman has taught me to accept my glass as half full. I have learnt to treat obstacles, hindrances, handicaps, setbacks and the unexpected as opportunities to profit from. If moving your body for a distance of 226km within 17 hours were a smooth journey then the race would not be called Ironman. Obstacles, big and small, the expected and the unexpected will confront you every step of the way. Rough seas, cold water, strong currents and tides and jellyfish await you in the swim. Beside these, there are also a 1000 pairs of thrashing limbs fighting for space that isn't there. The hilly roads on the bike course, the strong winds, the furnace of hot and humid weather and thunderstorms are all part of the challenges you must face. No point swearing at Mother

Nature or cursing yourself for getting suckered into doing the race. You have two choices. Quit or continue. Quitting is easy, but to continue you have to deal with each and every obstacle that stands in your path. Can't get over it? Then figure a way to negotiate around it. It is a level playing field. Every participant faces the same hurdle. The Chinese words for crisis are made of two characters that make up one word 'danger and opportunity'. SO for every crisis there are opportunities. Crisis or opportunity, it is how you look at it.

I used to get rather mad when I suffered a flat tyre during a race. I would curse. I would swear. I would kick my bike. I soon learnt my actions were counterproductive and would serve only to hinder my progress of fixing the flat tyre. With an angry mind I would fumble and take twice the time to replace a new tube. Flat tyres and breakdowns are part and parcel of the challenges the sport presents. This is the reason we carry spare tubes, pumps, and repair kits. I have learnt to react differently now. I take a drink and then proceed to carry out the systematic process in fixing a flat. It saves time and also gives my legs the opportunity to rest while I was on the job. With the flat fixed, I continue the race with relief, a sense of accomplishment and fresher legs and mind, all for the loss of some 10-15 minutes that I might be able to recoup as the race progressed.

Once or twice a year I get sick usually during periods of high volume training, high mileage workouts and high intensity. My sickness nearly always would be upper respiratory. When my immune system is down during these times I would inflame the situation by getting aggravated and stressed at being sick. I would act uptight and restless and try to continue training through the illness or start training again before I was completely 100%. This only served to prolong my illness. Having learnt to accept this as part of the unavoidable training process, if I get sick now I take the rest I need to recover. I let my battered muscles and joints repair. I catch up with sleep. I read and do things I may have missed out on. Needless to say I recover much faster.

The Age Handicap

The classification of categories for most athletic events is usually divided under the following: elites who race for their country and or money, juniors and kids aged 18 and below and then the rest (age groupers from 18 to 80 plus). Many events break down the categories into competitive 5 year blocks. My current category is 75-79 for an Ironman race. In a local race I am in the 50 plus age group, which leaves me at a distinct disadvantage with so many younger and faster men in the same group. This very fact acts as a deterrent to similar old timers such as myself and they stop competing or taking part. I, however, take the handicap differently. I race to have fun, to test myself against Mother Nature and against the clock. Being the oldest and the 'grandpa' of the lot I am always expected to be one of the last few, if not the last to cross any finish line. The reality however is far different. I usually end up beating a quarter of the field. So I race with no pressure, which is a great advantage. My usual strategy to a race is to hang at the back of the pack and stay clear of the stampede and not rush into the water for the swim start. I take my time to warm up and find my own rhythm. Then I begin to move through the field catching the slower swimmers. I enjoy the thrill and satisfaction in chasing and catching up with the juniors and those 60 and below. By the time I start the run my motivation is at its peak. And the icing on my cake is the pleasure of seeing the shock and panicky look on the faces of those I overtake, especially that of my late good friend Dr. Tan. "Where did grandpa come from?" Everyone I pass on the way to the finish line is a bonus to me as they are light years my junior. Where is the age handicap? It is how you take it. My glass is half full. The only handicap is in your head if you let it fester.

Lessons in humanity

I despise cold weather, especially cold water with the only exception being cold beer. I am a reasonably self-taught confident swimmer but throw me into cold water and I struggle. I signed up for Ironman Cairns in Australia thinking the swim would be in reasonably warm water like Kona, Hawaii or Tahiti where I had competed before. I was drawn in by the advertisement of 'tropical' Queensland not realizing that the race date in June signalled the beginning of winter in the Southern Hemisphere. I travelled to Cairns feeling in good condition and ready for the race.

The one thing I was unprepared for was the unexpected cold weather. When I landed at Cairns airport it was raining. I soon learnt that it had been raining the whole week with unusually cold winds. Race morning arrived and there was no change in the weather. The sea temperature was a wetsuit legal 23 degrees C. I had no wetsuit with me, having used one just once for a 750metre swim. I had trained for months for this race and spent a fair chunk of dollars to get there. I was not prepared to become a spectator on race day.

The race was a deep-water start, without a wetsuit to help keep me warm and conserve energy by helping me tread water I opted to stay on dry land before entering the water. This tactic may have kept me warmer but I was unable to warm up and the shock of jumping into the icy water upon the gun firing was a huge shock to my system. I immediately felt this was a bad omen. My swim did not go well right from the start but I still managed to get myself round the first lap in less than one hour. By the second lap however I was experiencing double vision and kept misreading the marker buoys (there were different colours for the buoys going out and coming in).

I have been doing triathlon so long that I know my old body well and how it functions right down to when I need my first pee! To save time I will usually pee 2-300 metres before reaching shore to save going to the portaloo in T1, but as hard as I tried I could not do it. Reaching the swim finish I had trouble climbing up the ramp, trembling all over, my teeth chattering, a race marshal pulled me up and took one look at me and then announced those words every athlete dreads to hear. "Sorry, but I cannot let you continue on." I was directed to the medical tent and found out that my core temperature had dropped below 34 degrees C and my heart rate was 60bpm. A medic wrapped me up with two towels reinforced with an aluminium foil on top and led me out to sit in the warm sun. He checked my temperature at regular intervals but was surprised to find no change. My bladder felt like it was bursting but I still could not pee. It was a terrible feeling. Finally a waiter at a nearby café having observed the condition I was in was kind enough to offer me a large cup of hot coffee. It immediately helped my body gain heat and I asked to be released from the medical tent.

Waiting at the shuttle bus stand wrapped in two sheets of aluminium foil like a Sunday Roast dinner I pondered my next move. The event is point-to-point meaning that the finish line where my wife was waiting was a long way away. The next shuttle bus to the hotel was three hours away and my wife was not expecting me until the evening. I only had AUD$17 with me, the remaining of my taxi fare from that morning. I was still in my tri-suit and a cheap T-Shirt to keep me warmer would cost eight bucks. The balance was not enough to buy me a cheap brunch. What should I do? It was then that I felt a tap on my shoulder. I turned around and there was a couple standing behind me. The lady handed me a black T-shirt still in the wrapper and walked on without waiting to acknowledge my thank you. I must have looked rather odd and miserable in the condition I was in to prompt such a kindly action.

I walked on to a nearby café where I ordered a tuna croissant and cappuccino. Before I was served the waitress gave me a mug of hot chocolate. Fearing I might not have enough money to pay for my order I told the waitress I did not order the drink. "It's okay. This is on the house to warm you up a bit while we prepare your food," she said. What could I say? I was floored by both acts of kindness in the space of 10 minutes. My DNF may have been a disappointment but it was nothing compared to the experience I gained out of the race. Now that was a real life lesson on humanity.

I know I should have left my tale of Lessons in Humanity there with a pleasant ending. But following the bitter and frustrating experience I have since gone through from my bike accident on January 17th 2016, I have learnt pleasant endings are not always going to happen. At some point through life you will be let down.

A Japanese woman called Mika Nakamura was driving the car that hit me from behind on that fateful day. Nakamura is in her 50's and has lived in Malaysia for over 18 years with a son and a daughter both studying in an international school.

Immediately post accident she was in shock and very apologetic showing great concern and insisted on taking me to a hospital and make a police report. She assured me she would bear all my medical expenses and pay for the cost of repair to my bike.

I too was in shock, perhaps more so than her and in a complete daze of all that had just happened. I felt numb and I did not accept her immediate offer. It was past midday and I was thirsty and hungry and just wanted to get home. Despite my injuries, I did not feel much pain, adrenalin must have kicked in and it was not until a few days after the accident that I started feeling the pain physically, consequences of such an ordeal.

My broken bike could not fit into her small car so she drove me home, leaving her teenage daughter to carry my bike and walk the kilometre to the entrance of the resort where my house is situated. When she left she gave me her business card. I was taken in or rather misled by her gesture. I had no reason to doubt her honesty, as other drivers would have fled from the scene.

After receiving the photos detailing the damages to my bike she texted me:

"Yes, I receive picture. Please send me the invoice after repair. Money no problem. I am worry about your body."

My bike frame was a carbon fibre custom made Guru. Damaged beyond repair. I paid S$8000 for it in 2006. I depreciated its value down by half to S$4000 from which I proposed we bear half each. So her share is S$2000 x 2.4 which was the exchange rate in 2000 (over three at the time of accident). The rear derailleur of the Shimano electronic gears shifter was also damaged. The supplier would not sell the part separately except the complete set at RM4200 which was what I paid six months before the accident. I proposed she bear half of the cost. This together with my medical expenses came to RM7831. I submitted for her consideration. My medical expenses have since gone up as my treatment is ongoing. I did not want the matter to drag on any further fearing memory may fade with time. I even asked her to consult her insurance claim adjuster and compensate me based on his recommendation or based on her conscience after failing to hear from her.

After calling a couple times to check on the status I finally got an email reply from her. She assured me she would take full responsibility but was unable to take care of the matter 'right now'. "My daughter is hospitalized in Japan and scheduled to come back only at the beginning of March. Can you wait until then?"

Well I waited until April 9. Again I asked her to compensate me for what she felt is comfortable with and I was met with silence. There was not even a word from her since.

This compelled me to let her know I might seek other available options to state my case, one of which is to give her a mention in this book to expose the ugly side of humanity. I am not being vengeful. My proposed claim was more than fair considering she was at fault. It is a fraction of what the accident cost me financially, physically and mentally.

Now, eight months post accident, I am still not the man I was before that day. I still suffer from nagging pain in my right ankle, right shoulder and left wrist. This woman almost single-handedly retired me to pasture from my only passion left in life. Her actions have truly shown me the ugly side of humanity is well and truly alive.

Father time

When I turned 70 I began to feel the effects of my age catching up with me. It became harder to go for long training sessions and harder to do high intensity workouts, both of which are integral to a triathlete's training regime. It was starting to take longer for my body to recover after each workout and I experienced aches and pains in parts of my body ALL of the time. I noticed my medical bills to sports clinics and doctors escalated too. The doctor told me that he could not help me any more unless I agreed to slow down. Slow down? My mind had yet to catch up with my body. Mentally I was in my mid 50's early 60's (on bad days). So the aches and pains became part of my life as I retreated into a cocoon of self-denial, then came 2009 when I achieved a personal best with a 14'46" at Ironman Malaysia in Langkawi. "Hey Doc! Who said I am old? Who said I couldn't improve with age?"

In October of the same year I went back to Kona, Hawaii harbouring hopes of bettering my personal best. My whole family came along. I was giving my son a Hawaiian wedding the day after the race. Alas, there was no PB for me but it was okay. Hawaii is always tough. And the lead up had seen me sidelined with severe lower back pain that resulted in my needing cortisone jabs just to get me on the start line. Despite the set back I was still in denial mode – I believe this is a mindset many triathletes share whatever their age! I decided to wait until Ironman Malaysia 2010 to have another shot at a personal best. February came round and I completed my 10th Ironman Malaysia. I had expected the Old Lady to give me a hug and tell me how proud she was that I had finished another Ironman. It was my fifteenth finish in as many years. Instead, on crossing the line I got an earful.

"What take you so long ah? I am so tired of waiting for you!"

"I am okay la," was my instant reply.

"Look at the clock!" she yelled at me.

I looked. It was past 11pm. My time of 16 hours and 11 minutes was my worst outing in Langkawi. The whole day I thought I was doing okay as my mind was telling me go, go, GO. Little did I realize I was stuck in first gear the entire race, it's a common problem with speed perception among old people. Yes. Maybe three Ironman in twelve months is a little too much to ask of this body.

My body has to live my Ironman dream. Father time has finally taken its toll on me. After I turned 75 the loss of body mass became more noticeable despite continuing to live an active lifestyle. Going the distance is tough enough at 50 or 60 or 70. At 75 the noticeable loss of muscular power really started to slow me down considerably and doing an Ironman became an ordeal. But it is an ordeal I am prepared to endure. I know its still possible since I have a good endurance base. However, it is meeting the various cut-off times that pose a real challenge, but hey, Ironman is about ordinary people performing extraordinary feats thought impossible. I am exploring new training methods to drive my body forward more efficiently and effectively.

Ironman Malaysia 2014 blew my previous worst timing out of the park. I came home in 16 hours and 51 minutes. Now this is my record slowest time. This time around there was no earful from the Old Lady.

In fact she was relieved I made it. Reality finally struck me. I am old, but the Ox in me WILL NOT QUIT.

At Ironman Malaysia 2015 I missed the bike cut off by over 45 minutes. This was my first DNF in all twelve starts at Ironman Malaysia. My perfect finisher record had come to an end. Two days before the race I was officially inducted into the Ironman Malaysia Hall of Fame during the welcoming dinner for all participants. I am the first Malaysian, and perhaps the first Asian to receive such an honour; a status I never dreamed of. I have fought and paid with my sweat, my tears, my pain and my blood. It can never be bought not even with all the money in the world. I proudly brought my entire family, including my son's in-laws to witness my induction and celebrate the occasion. The icing on the cake would have been my twelfth finish and the perfect occasion to perhaps roll down the final curtain on my Ironman journey. But, alas, sadly there was no Bollywood ending for me. So what next?

The answer was simple and it arrived on January 9th, 2016. I received an email from the World Triathlon Corporation titled "Congratulations on becoming a 2016 Ironman Silver All World Athlete!" Despite a bad year, my performance during 2015 had positioned me in the top 5% of my age group earning me Silver All World Athlete Status.

Gold signifies the top 1%. I move up to the 80 and above age group next year so that title could be in my reach. Maybe I should have one more shot before hitting the road?

Wake-up! Doubting Thomases – Anything is Possible

Late in the afternoon of Sunday 8 May 2016 an awards party was in full swing in the ground of Hyatt Regency Hotel, Da-Nang Vietnam. The music was loud, the beers free flowing and Whit Raymond, the event's lead emcee, who has called my name countless times over the past years, was dancing in between announcing the results.

As the eldest in the field of 1100 plus athletes I had the 'honour' of being the last to go on stage to receive my first place trophy. (I was the only one in the 75-79 age category). I had to go down on both knees to climb on to the podium due to countless bottles of Budweiser I had consumed since crossing the finish line earlier that afternoon.

It appears I had become something of a celebrity being the eldest athlete and was propositioned numerous times for photos. Each time someone came up and asked for a photo I was offered a fresh beer as a trade of sorts which I accepted of course as it would be rude to refuse, right?

So when it came to my time to be up on stage the only thing I remember is Whit asking how I felt and how did I do it? He like many others was aware that I was rehabilitating from my bike accident in January. "It is truly amazing," he said.

So there I was soaking up the fun and party atmosphere when Wong Hock Yim, a friend and fellow participant, brought to my attention my trophy was blank with no inscription. Disappointed I immediately confronted the race organiser. The look of shock and moment of awkwardness on her face made me smile, I had the last laugh. I suspect the trophy was meant for another podium finisher in a different age group and they didn't actually make one for my age group as, perhaps they didn't think I could finish? I wasn't even the last to finish! The inscribed plate was removed hastily and the blank trophy handed to me. She promised to mail me a new plate with the correct inscription.

Upon receipt of my registration for the race early this year, the Race Secretariat requested re-confirmation of my birth date. Besides providing the proof, I also informed them I competed the same race in 2015 as a 78 years old. I missed the cut-off by less than two minutes. 2015 was a bad year in my Ironman journey. I raced Ironman Malaysia for the 12th time, but missed the bike cut-off resulting in my first DNF in 12 starts. I also raced four other 70.3, [including Vietnam] the same year. Three of these races took place within two months and two days. This is a big ask for most people so rather a tall order for this 78 year-old. For the first time in my life I suffered from dehydration during the first race in Subic Bay, Philippines. Somehow I managed to drag myself to the finish but missed the cut-off by about two minutes. This setback might have affected my other races in that year. Oh, for sure, father time threw more than just a spanner in my works last year.

In 2013, I raced a 70.3 in Cebu, Philippines winning my age category

(75-79) in 7 hours 33 minutes. But there was no trophy for me. There I was standing on the podium with both my hands raised for the photos, minus the trophy. I am not sure who was more embarrassed, me, or Geoff Meyer the then CEO of Ironman Asia-Pacific (now MD of Ironman Asia) who was supposed to present the trophy or two other officials on stage. The trophy came by post the following week.

All these events were organised and staged by companies under Sunrise Events Inc. Philippines. Yet they screwed me up time and time again and it bugs me. Maybe they never expected this old man to finish the race. As my age creeps towards 80, it becomes progressively tougher to race the Ironman. Besides having to contend with father time, I have to deal with an increasing number of doubting Thomases, aka organizers who, it seems, bet against me making the finish line of their races.

For Ironman 70.3 Vietnam, I raced with more than just the challenge of a 79 year-old body. I was half trained due to slow rehabilitation from my bike accident. I still have nagging pain in my right ankle and need painkillers on race morning to get me started. So I went into the race with no expectation, and no pressure. It was a test case to see if my body could hold up to go the distance. My take is, when under trained, you carry no expectations. You have no pressure, so give your best and soak up the fun and the result may surprise you. It could be just the occasion for you to pop open a bottle of champagne at the finish line. When over trained with high expectation and pressure, your race day could turn out to be a miserable one. Your cocoon is nearby.

Epilogue

What started out as a small mission to get back into shape, following the advice from my doctor, transformed into a lifelong journey of self-discovery and self-development. From the routine workouts in the gym, slow jogs around the Subang Ria Lake, into training, purposeful training and now into specific training, turned me into an endurance freak and endorphin junkie. Thirty years into endurance sports, 27 years racing the triathlons and following the Ironman dream for 21 years have taught me to always expect the unexpected. My induction into the Ironman Malaysia Hall of Fame is totally unexpected. A big, big surprise and what an honour, fought and paid with my sweat, my tears, my pain and my blood. This cannot be bought even if I have all the money in the world. It can never be taken away unlike titles given or bought.

I have a love-hate relationship with the Ironman dating back 21 years from October 1995. Love, there's are little, but hate aplenty. Seeking fame was never in my mind when I plunged into the Pacific Ocean at

7.00 am on a Saturday morning of October 7, 1995, Kona, Hawaii. It was the first of my 20 attempts in the Ironman at a tender age of 58, relatively speaking due to my late start of the sport. Many at my age would have retired from their work and been enjoying their golden years, but I just started my journey. I was drawn into the sport by the extraordinary and almost inhuman feats by ordinary people. Wow! That is fantastic. I want to do that. The bumble bee in me tells me I can do it. Jumping into the sea that morning was my way of finding out if I had what it takes to go the distance despite my zero background in the three disciplines. Well, you never know if you never try. The key ingredients here are 'think like a bumble bee, train like a racehorse'. Believe in yourself and train with the single mindedness of a race horse. Now, 21 years on, I am still at it, following the same dream. Now at 79, the job ahead is much more herculean.

I did three Ironman in 10 months when I was 63. Nine years later at 72, I did another three in 12 months. Two of these were in Kona Hawaii, the world championship. I finished all of them hitting my personal best at 14 hours 46 minutes in Langkawi in 2009 at 72 years of age. It was my most memorable race. I spent the whole day and a big part of the night hunting down a Japanese competitor who had beaten me by over 1 hr 20 mins four years back. I finally caught and passed him on the 2nd loop of the five loops of the marathon. It was the race of my life. So it is possible to improve with age if you do it right. Now in my twilight years and at the tail end of my journey, racing the Ironman once a year is a struggle. Struggle it may be, but racing one Ironman, one 70.3 plus one to two Olympic distance triathlons a year still leave me a little restless. The old body is no longer able and willing, but the brain still needs more of the feel good endorphin. Early last year, I did three 70.3 in two months and two days, followed by a fourth one three months later. They almost kill me. 70.3 or the half Ironman as it was called before, though tough, is very much doable in my book. I think I have done more than 35 such races over the years. I even raced one in Tahiti the year the staging of Ironman Malaysia was in limbo. I travelled for two days for a seven hours race. Such is the grip the Ironman has on me. As recent as 2014, I still manage one with almost an hour to spare before the cut-off. My decline this year is both dramatic and drastic. Father time really tore into me. I can hear my alarm ringing. Many people my age need walking stick to move around. How am I to move mine for 226km without one and meet the various cut-off times? Shooting for a new **PR** is now but a pipe dream. Going the distance and meeting the cut-offs are both stressful and painful – a huge mountain to scale. Still I will continue regardless. Giving up will be game over for me.

Ironman is 37 last October. It is still a young sport. There are limited records and information for us, the oldies in our late 70s to lean on and learn how to move an ageing body. Oh, sure, there are good coaches out there, but few, if any, have experience racing successfully in their 70s and are still around to impart their knowledge. So the handful of us, the stubborn and the crazies are left to explore new frontiers, to find ways and means to move the old body. Ironman is about one daring to take that step beyond, into the unknown. We are now on the same path taken by the 15 pioneers 38 years back. Led by US navy commander John Collins, the founder, these brave people went into the unknown and came back to tell the world the Ironman is doable. As multiple finishers and in our sunset years, we are on the same path to prove that the Ironman is still doable even at an advanced age. Turning the clock back may not be possible in the foreseeable future and not in my lifetime, but slowing it down is within reach. I have no doubt one of us will succeed in unlocking the secret one day. To go fast after 80. It is possible. "Anything is possible", if you are an Ironman.

Receiving my Ironman Malaysia Hall of Fame award at the Langkawi Ironman 2015.

Celebrating my induction to the Ironman Malaysia Hall of Fame with my family. From left to right: Joyce, my in-laws, Sheila, Ethan (my grandson), Ivi (my daughter-in-law), Evynne (my granddaughter) and Rodney.

My collection of finisher's medals over the years.

Anything is possible, if you are an Ironman.

Printed in Dunstable, United Kingdom